# BREAK OUT

Also by Graeme Cook

*None But the Valiant:*
EXCITING TRUE WAR STORIES IN THE AIR AND AT SEA

*Commandos in Action*

# BREAK OUT

## *FAMOUS MILITARY ESCAPES OF THE WORLD WARS*

Graeme Cook

*Taplinger Publishing Company*
*New York*

First published in the United States in 1974 by
TAPLINGER PUBLISHING CO., INC.
New York, New York



LIBRARY OF CONGRESS CATALOGING IN PUBLICATION DATA:

Cook, Graeme.
Breakout; famous military escapes of the World Wars.
New York: Taplinger Publishing Company, 1974.
~~Bibliography:~~ 189 p.
1. World War, 1939–1945—Prisoners and prisons.
2. European War, 1914–1918—Prisoners and prisons.
3. Escapes. I. Title.

D805.A2C63 940.5'47 74-3871

ISBN 0-8008-0968-8

To Susan

# *Contents*

# *Acknowledgements*

I would like to express my sincere gratitude to all the authors and publishers who so kindly granted me permission to draw upon their works for much of the information contained in this book. Without their willing co-operation, this book could not have been written.

Special thanks are also due to the following people whose generous assistance made writing this book so much easier—the Director and staff of the Imperial War Museum, London; the Curator and staff of the Royal Air Force Museum, Hendon; Valerie Furniss; Vic and June Parry; Bryan Philpott; the Chief Librarian and staff of Newbury Public Library; Michael Stevens; Reet Nelis; Anita Pollack and many others.

G.C.

# *Introduction*

On the night of 24 March 1944, seventy-six Allied Air Force officers escaped from the prisoner-of-war camp, Stalag Luft III, at Sagan, in Germany. Of the men who scrambled from the tunnel mouth that night only three succeeded in returning safely to Britain. The others were recaptured and upon the orders of Adolf Hitler, the German Führer, fifty of them were murdered by the German secret police, the Gestapo.

That mass killing of escaping prisoners was in direct contravention of all the accepted rules governing the treatment of prisoners in wartime and it was by no means an isolated incident in Germany. Others were executed while attempting to escape or on trumped-up charges of espionage, as will be seen in the chapters which follow.

The business of escaping from captivity in time of war was by no stretch of the imagination a thrilling adventure, as some misguided story-tellers would have us believe. It was a highly dangerous undertaking. The running escaper, perhaps a pilot who had bombed a German city and helped reduce it to ruins, killing men, women and children in the process, could expect little mercy from the civilian population if he were caught during his attempt to flee their country. There are cases on record of crashed Allied bomber crews being murdered by civilians before the military could reach them. When the tide of war was running against the enemy the fugitive was invariably faced with a hostile population bent on revenge.

When a prisoner took it upon himself to escape from Germany, particularly during the latter stages of the war, he was risking not only recapture and a lengthy term of solitary confinement in a camp gaol but his own life and indeed the lives of others who might have helped him on his way. A nervous guard patrolling his beat along a camp wire would shoot first at the slightest suspicious movement on a dark night and few questions would be asked afterwards.

The stories of escapes from prisoner-of-war camps are grossly misleading if they imply that the escapers were dashing young cavaliers, hungry for adventure and only happy when they were faced with danger. These were ordinary men who found themselves in extra-ordinary situations with the same fears all of us have. They were desperate, hunted men often at large in hostile countries. They were invariably exhausted, hungry, tense and frightened men, who knew that every step they took might lead them back into the miserable hole they had escaped from or bring them a bullet.

During the two world wars of this century thousands of men attempted to escape from captivity—all but a few failed. Cunning, ingenuity, determination and courage but above all luck were the essentials of successful escape and without any of these, failure was inevitable. The chapters which follow tell of some of the lucky ones and of some of those who were not so lucky: of men like Jan Baalsrud who was hunted across the frozen and mountainous wastes of Arctic Norway; of Warrant Officer Grimson who escaped no less than six times but relinquished freedom to remain in occupied territory and help others to escape; of Charles McCormac who fled from a Japanese prisoner-of-war camp and lived off the jungle; of Oberleutnant Franz von Werra, a young German pilot who caused havoc in Britain and almost wrecked the British system of prisoner interrogation; and of Lieutenant A. J. Evans, one of the most determined escapers of the First World War, a man who would not be caged ...

# 1

# *Escape from Germany*

Of the many thousands of British soldiers, sailors and airmen taken prisoner by the enemy during the First World War, most of them thought at one time or another of escape. Many tried but few succeeded. Some, having tried to break out once and failed, gave up in despair. Others resigned themselves to imprisonment for the duration of the war, occupying themselves in studies of one sort or another to while away the agonisingly long days. But for some, like Lieutenant A. J. Evans of the Royal Flying Corps, the thought of escape never left them for a conscious moment.

On 1 July 1916, the bloody Somme Offensive opened with the thundering roar of hundreds of heavy guns raining shells down upon the teeming thousands of German and Allied soldiers. Day and night the battle raged, taking its toll, while above this hell on earth flew the 'eyes' of the army, the artillery spotter planes which directed the fire of heavy guns on to their targets. Lieutenant A. J. Evans, of No. 3 Squadron R.F.C., was among those who flew over the shell-ravaged countryside, spying out the land for the gunners, flashing back the positions and range of enemy artillery emplacements to the gunners then watching the missiles pound their targets to destruction.

Early on the morning of 10 July, Evans and his observer, Lieutenant Long, took off from their base on a reconnaissance mission over the German lines. The frail aircraft climbed high into the sky until it reached 4,000 feet and the two men set about the task of seeking out the German emplacements but as the aircraft cruised over a point about ten miles north-east of Bapaume the engine gave a cough and splutter then fell silent. Try as he might, Evans could not get her to re-start. Almost instantly the aircraft began to lose height. There was no hope of reaching the British lines and as the aircraft glided towards the ground Evans' eyes searched for a suitable place to land, preferably near a wood into which they could dash after they had set fire to their machine. Above all they had to make sure the machine was destroyed so that it did not fall into German hands.

But then as they neared the ground they saw that it was alive with enemy troops and a German rocket battery opened up at them sending rockets whipping into the air at them. Luckily it was far from accurate and Evans managed to dodge them as they came zooming skywards but they diverted his attention from finding a landing place.

Evans' aircraft had reached two hundred feet before he finally spotted an open space dead ahead of him. The landing was to be tricky but there was another problem—a German gun battery was sighted there and Evans knew that he wouldn't have time to set fire to his aircraft before the German troops reached him. There was only one thing for it. He would have to crash the aircraft. He swept over a cluster of trees then, as the aircraft lost speed, he dipped the nose into the ground. It hit and crumpled into a tangled heap of wreckage leaving both Evans and Long hanging by their seat straps. They were dazed by the impact but instinctively struggled free of the plane. Evans was more aware of what was happening than Long who had been concussed by the crash and was staggering aimlessly around the wreckage. Although the plane was a write-off Evans was determined to finish the job and grabbed a box of matches which Long had ready, but already armed troops were rushing towards him. He struggled into the wreckage to find the petrol tap but before he could a German trooper arrived and waved the muzzle of his rifle in Evans' face. To continue would have meant a bullet. The hard-bitten front-line German soldier was not a man to tangle with. He saw death daily and killed as a matter of course, so one more dead Englishman would mean nothing to him. Evans, resigned to his fate, obligingly raised his arms in surrender.

With that a German officer arrived on the scene and ordered the two men to be searched. When he put his hand in his pocket, Evans found to his horror that he had his diary with him and it contained scribbled notes which could be of use to the enemy. He'd forgotten to leave it behind before taking off on the mission. At all costs the Germans must not get their hands on it, so instead of allowing them to search him, Evans volunteered to empty his own pockets and laid out his bits and pieces for the officer to see, carefully omitting to produce the diary. This seemed to satisfy the German who took possession of his belongings then he and Long were led off at rifle point. While they were being escorted to the German command post, Evans managed by sleight of hand to dispose of the diary. With that off his mind he turned his thoughts to escape but at this early juncture and under heavy guard, the prospect of pulling off a dash for freedom was out of the question.

Evans and Long were taken from the command headquarters and marched for several hours before reaching another building. Until then they had been treated with reluctant courtesy and a certain degree of respect but when they arrived at this other building there occurred an incident which could have had serious consequences. While they were sitting waiting for something to happen, a group of orderlies came into their room. They had heard that both men were British fliers and seemed hell-bent on murder. It appeared that a German hospital train had been bombed to destruction just a few days before and many of the wounded soldiers in it killed. The mistake of the British had been genuine since the train had not shown the required red cross and was therefore a legitimate target but this did nothing to allay the wrath of the German orderlies. They wanted revenge and for a moment things looked decidedly nasty until a German officer intervened and ordered them out of the room.

From there Evans and Long were taken by train to a fort at Cambrai where they stayed for six days during which time they were both interrogated. Although the food they were given was little short of appalling, their treatment was fair and considering their situation, they found little to complain of. Things were later to take a turn for the worse but in the meantime they were treated with consideration and even taken under escort to visit a neighbouring German Air Service base where they were shown over a Fokker squadron. The Germans evidently imagined that they had them 'in the bag' for the duration for if they did not, they certainly would not have allowed them the privilege of viewing their fighter base. Evans paid particular attention to the Germans' method of operation, vowing that if and when he got back to his own lines he would pass on the vital information. But before an escape attempt could be made they were transferred to a prisoner-of-war camp at Gütersloh.

On arrival at the camp, Evans was instantly aware of the overall air of depression amongst the internees and soon gathered that many of them had given up all hope of escape. The atmosphere was not helped by the thought that the camp had once been a lunatic asylum. The food dished up by the Germans was foul in the extreme and for the most part uneatable but small luxuries were obtainable. Wine and whisky could be bought at the camp canteen from the prisoners' allowance and there were tennis courts and a field for playing football. Indeed, when compared with camps in which Evans was later to find himself, this one bordered on Utopia. Their stay at Gütersloh was short and after about six weeks they, along with all the other R.F.C. officers, were transferred to a camp at Clausthal, in the Harz mountains, south of Hanover.

Immediately upon arrival, Evans began a systematic examination of the camp with a view to escape. It consisted of a large house which had formerly been an hotel and three barrack blocks, surrounded by a barbed wire entanglement. In another barbed wire enclosure were some tennis courts. The whole camp was heavily guarded by sentries, some who remained stationary while others prowled with dogs.

Evans had not been at Clausthal long when he learned that some of the prisoners were busy digging a tunnel from one of the barrack blocks. Two of the diggers had opted out of the scheme so Evans and a Belgian called Kicq were offered places in the team. Both jumped at the chance of being in on the act but Evans was somewhat dismayed when he saw the tunnel. It was planned to lead from the block nearest the fence under the wire and up at the other side but there was a major problem—it was partially waterlogged and working in it was extremely difficult. However, urged on by the thought of escape, Evans and his new-found Belgian friend went to work on it with a vengeance. It was tiring, back-breaking toil, labouring in the enclosed space, wet through and with little air to breathe but in spite of the appalling conditions they battled on. As the tunnel progressed, the air became so foul that fresh air had to be pumped in to the diggers by means of an improvised air-conditioning unit —a pair of bellows with a long pipe attached to them. This helped a little but did not prevent the digger from being overcome and passing-out at frequent intervals.

While they were not busily engaged in digging, Kicq and Evans schemed and plotted how, when they had escaped, they were to evade detection and reach friendly territory. There were several possibilities open to them but each of them had its dangers. It must be remembered that, unlike the prisoners of World War Two, the escaper of the Great War had not the experiences of past escapers to help him. He had to rely entirely on his own wits and inventiveness to escape so that although conditions in World War One camps were perhaps more bearable than those suffered by the prisoner of World War Two, the former had a more difficult problem facing him when his thoughts turned to escape.

Evans and Kicq were faced with two basic alternatives. They could either head for the Dutch or the Swiss borders. The former, they had been told by a reliable informant, was the more difficult since it was heavily guarded by sentries, lined with electric fences and for the most part patrolled by dog-handlers. The other escape route would involve crossing the Swiss border which seemed to be the more promising of the two, although it was very much farther away. It was less well guarded and the chances of crossing it without detection were correspondingly greater. The problem of how to get to the actual frontier was the greatest worry, although this did not seem to bother Kicq, who maintained that given a suitable set of civilian clothes, they could make the journey by train, passing themselves off as Germans or foreign workers. Both of them spoke the German language sufficiently well to do this. But a blow to their escape plans came when the tunnel had to be abandoned. It had become impossible to work in and the threat of a cave-in was growing daily.

Disappointed but not disheartened, Evans and Kicq looked around for another means of escape. During this time, Evans made a point of befriending one of the German guards who seemed a likely candidate for bribery. He could not have made a more fortunate choice. Within a few days, the guard had given him a mass of information on train travel throughout Germany together with other bits and pieces of information which would be helpful to an escaper. Furthermore he had agreed to help Evans escape, providing he was in no way implicated. In return, Evans promised, upon his successful return to Britain, to deposit 500 marks in a bank for the German's wife. Things were looking up and it was with growing excitement that Evans scoured the camp for a way out. One day while walking round the wire, he found it.

Close by the wire at a point near the house was a garden patch with thick shrubs, bushes and vegetables. The bushes were so dense that the fence at that point could not be seen from the inside of the camp although it could be watched by patrolling sentries outside the wire. The fact that it was obscured at least in part gave them half a chance of getting out unobserved at night. Evans already knew where he could get a pair of wire-cutters and with these he planned to cut through the fence then make a bolt for it when the time was right. He told Kicq of his plan and the Belgian jumped at the idea of going along with him.

Word of proposed escapes travelled fast among the prisoners of Clausthal, and Evans learned that two other prisoners had the same idea so they pooled their resources and decided to make the break together. Between the four of them, they rustled up as much German money as they could find and scrounged what civilian clothing they could from other inmates. What they lacked in clothing they improvised by dyeing parts of their uniforms, taking off belts and replacing military buttons. Within a few days all four of them had a suit of clothes.

Every day they kept a watch on the garden patch discovering the routine of the patrolling sentries, the length of their 'beats' and how long it took them to walk from point A to point B. Timing was vital for they had to know exactly how long a sentry's back would be turned so that they could bolt for cover outside the wire. They discovered that there was really only one sentry who had a clear view of their escape point and the break would have to be made when he was at the farthest part of his beat if they were to reach cover without being seen. The greatest worry, however, was not the sentry but 'stray' Germans who used the path alongside the fence to reach the guardhouse only twenty or so yards away.

When the appointed time for the break came at dusk one evening, the compound was teeming with prisoners, strolling about in groups in semi-darkness. Among them were the four would-be escapers, all clad in their escape clothes. This was not such an audacious display as one might imagine since many of the prisoners were clad in a weird assortment of civilian and military clothes.

They tried as best they could to remain inconspicuous and wandered seemingly aimlessly towards the garden. As they passed it one of them, Ding by name, slid into the bushes, clutching the wire-cutters and began work on the fence. Only a second after he made the first cut, a sentry passed within inches of him and he scrambled back and out of the garden. He thought he had been seen and it was indeed miraculous that he had not, considering the noise he made during his retreat through the bushes, but in fact the German had not spotted him. The resulting excitement was such that they decided to postpone their attempt until another night and made their way back to their barracks. But once there, Ding found that he had left his greatcoat by the wire fence. If it were discovered, it would certainly give the game away and ruin any further chances they might have of using the same exit. Nichol, Ding's partner, very gallantly went back and rescued the greatcoat.

Evans and Kicq decided after due debate to wait for another week before making an attempt, but in the meantime the others decided to drop out of the venture. Nichol, however, agreed to cut the wire for the two escapers, thus lessening the chance of their getting dirty in the attempt. During the week that followed they again discussed their routine and decided, after due consideration and the advice of others, to alter their escape route. Instead of heading for Switzerland, they would travel by train from Goslar to Düsseldorf and there try to bribe a Dutch bargee to take them into Holland in his barge. This seemed to them to be the simplest way of doing it, providing of course that they could find a bargee willing to take them. If they couldn't, then they would have to risk crossing the frontier on foot. But since their very venture was fraught with danger they decided to risk it.

Seven nights later they made their way to the break-out point as before and Nichol got to work on the wire. Within a few minutes he was out of the patch.

'It's cut,' he said urgently. 'Good luck!' With that he mingled again with the other prisoners and Evans and Kicq took one last look round to see that the coast was clear before ducking in amongst the bushes. They scrambled through them until they got to the fence and peered through the gap. Not far from them was a sentry standing motionless when he should have been marching. 'Damn him!' they thought, but in a few seconds he shouldered his rifle and marched off on his beat with his back to them. Then was their time to move.

Kicq was first through and Evans shoved through his haversack crammed with food and provisions. Then he too scrambled through the gap in the wire and the two men bolted into the darkness behind the arc lamps which played on the compound. They ran with all their might, covering a hundred yards in record time before pausing to catch their breath. While they stood, they listened for the sound of pursuers but all was quiet. The alarm had not been raised and from where they stood they could still see the sentries under the arc lights marching along their beats. They'd done it. After a whispered exchange of congratulations they made off deeper into the night. It was by then 7 p.m. and ahead of them was a long walk to Goslar station where they were to catch the train. Off they tramped through the night, making good time as they went but moving with caution. If luck were with them, their escape would not be discovered until morning but there was a chance of walking headlong into trouble if they did not tread warily. They trudged on, carefully avoiding houses and cottages on their route by giving them a wide berth. Now and again they stopped to check their bearings with the aid of two compasses which had been specially manufactured for them in the camp.

Evans and Kicq made such good progress that they were way ahead of schedule when they caught sight of the lights at Goslar. The last thing they wanted to do was arrive early and spend time waiting at the station. This would lay them open to discovery. They wanted to buy their tickets at the last possible moment before the train was due to depart, so they lay in hiding for a good half hour before making their way into the town. Now, they realised, would be the telling time. It was two o'clock in the morning and there were a few people about which made it impossible to remain inconspicuous. They would soon find out if their improvised clothes did the trick.

They walked briskly but without undue haste through the town, passing only a few people, none of whom gave them more than a casual glance. Then they came to the railway station where they made their way into the booking office.

As they had previously arranged, they entered the booking office separately, the idea being that if one of them were caught the other would at least have a chance of escape. They also agreed that from then on, neither one would recognise the other, no matter what happened and above all they would keep as far away as possible from each other. If the alarm had by then been raised, the hunters would be looking for two men together so it was best to remain apart for as long as they could to avoid suspicion.

Kicq walked boldly up to the ticket desk and bought his ticket for Düsseldorf and after a suitable time had elapsed, during which Evans studied the time-table, he too marched up to the desk and bought his. The encounter with the official was not, however, without its moment of tension. Evans asked for a single to Düsseldorf but before he got it the clerk muttered something to him which he did not catch. Evans, in a bid to remain offhand, gave the clerk an extra five marks but he had misunderstood the clerk and the official looked at him curiously, wondering why the man had made such a silly mistake. The clerk had merely asked if he had the right change. The man gave Evans back his five marks together with his ticket but it was little slip-ups like that which could spell disaster for Evans and from then on he determined to be more cautious.

Evans made his way on to the platform where he saw Kicq striding purposefully up and down. He kept his distance, eyeing the other passengers all the time for any hint of suspicion. Evans felt that every German on that station platform was watching him, suspecting him and just about to raise the alarm. He wondered if he had been missed at the camp; if already the countryside were teeming with soldiers looking for him and Kicq and whether at any moment a posse of soldiers might burst on to the platform and arrest both of them. But his fears were unfounded and at last the train pulled into the station.

Evans made for the third-class section of the train and in doing so lost sight of Kicq. He wasn't to see him again for some time and then it was to be in prison. It transpired that Kicq found himself in a compartment with a German officer with whom he was obliged to get into conversation and although he put up a valiant effort at deception, his identity was eventually discovered and he was arrested and thrown once more back into the bag. Evans, however, had better luck . . .

When he boarded the train he went in search of a seat, one preferably in which he could go to sleep—or at least pretend to, to avoid getting into conversation with anyone. But he found to his horror that the train was packed with soldiers and most of the seats were reserved for them. But at last he found a corner seat where he buried himself in a newspaper he'd bought at the station, then pretended to go to sleep.

So far the journey was without incident for Evans. He had no knowledge of the fate of Kicq and assumed that he too was enjoying the same degree of success. At last the train pulled into Düsseldorf at about eight-thirty in the morning and Evans got off. He scanned the platform for a sign of his friend but Kicq was nowhere to be seen. Evans dared not hang about so he made his way into the main waiting hall and for some ten minutes sat waiting for his friend but he did not come. Something had obviously happened to him and if that were the case, Evans too was in danger of being discovered. Regrettably he had to leave Kicq to his own devices and made his way out of the station. As he was leaving, he bought a map of the city from a nearby bookstall. It was while he was doing this that he spotted a uniformed official eyeing him curiously. Evans didn't like the look of him at all and suspected that he had tumbled to his identity. This was no place to linger so he hurriedly left.

With the aid of his map he made his way to the docks where he surveyed the ships, boats and barges but there were no Dutch ones to be seen. After an exhaustive search he could not find what he wanted and made up his mind to try for the border and take pot luck at getting over the frontier into Holland. This was to be far from easy. He had no proper map of that part of Germany, and with only a compass to guide him, he would in all probability land himself in hot water. Anyone found wandering aimlessly around the border was immediately suspect. Somehow he had to get a map and he could think of no other way of getting one than buying it.

Taking the bull by the horns he walked boldly into a shop and asked for a map of the area between Crefeld and the frontier. The female shop assistant did not think she had such a thing and summoned her husband who turned out to be a German army corporal. Evans was taken aback when he saw the man in uniform but he determined to lie his way out of the situation. The corporal explained that he couldn't sell a map to just anyone. There were so many spies and escaped prisoners about that it was dangerous to part with a map of the frontier. If only he'd known, thought Evans. Summoning up his best German he tried to be as casual as he could and explained that he was on a walking holiday but had no good map of the area. This seemed to satisfy the German and he parted with an excellent map, exactly what Evans wanted. With that Evans inwardly heaved a sigh of relief and wasted no time in getting out of the shop and into the street where he made off at a quick pace.

By then he was hungry and he found a public park where he sat and ate some of his food while he studied his map and considered where he should go from there. He knew from a time-table, which he had bought with the map, that there was a tram service from Düsseldorf to Crefeld and he decided to take this. At least, he thought, it would get him closer to his target, the frontier, then he would have to see how the land lay from there. Having made the decision, he packed his things and was just doing so when he noticed an old man watching him closely. From the way he acted, the old man was obviously suspicious of Evans and when the German walked behind a bush, Evans dodged behind another out of sight of the man and then darted through a shrubbery into a road where he jumped on a passing tram. He glanced through the window and there was the old man hot on his heels but by getting on the tram he'd given him the slip. Had he waited he was sure the old man would have given the game away and had him arrested. After a short spell, Evans alighted from the tram and made his way along the river and into the city to the tram terminus. He had not been there long when a tram arrived.

Evans found a seat but then the conductress approached and he discovered that he had boarded the wrong tram. The conductress showed no signs of suspicion and advised him to get off at the next stop and wait for the tram that followed. This he did and opposite the tram stop he spotted a beer hall which he entered and asked for a glass of beer. The beer arrived and he gave the waitress a mark to pay for it but just then he saw his tram coming and made off into the street and leapt on it just as it was pulling away. At that the waitress came racing after him, waving frantically. For a moment he thought that she had tumbled to him. But it dawned on him that he'd forgotten to pick up his change and he yelled back to the woman to keep it. He'd had two too many close shaves for the day and it was with some relief that he sat back in his seat and tried to relax.

The tram journey passed without incident and he arrived at the Crefeld terminus. In many ways it was a strange experience for him being there because he knew that his brother, who had been wounded and taken prisoner, was in captivity in a prisoner-of-war camp somewhere in Crefeld. How curious it would be, he thought, if he were to see his brother. But he had to sweep that dangerous possibility from his mind. If he did see his brother, he would instantly recognise him and the game could well be up for Evans.

Throughout the entire town there were obvious signs of a camp nearby. Prison guards were in evidence in every street as Evans walked along them and he occasionally spotted groups of French prisoners being marched off to work in the fields and factories.

At last he reached the outskirts of the town and made his way into the country, where possible avoiding passing through villages. He was completely worn out after his night's adventures and decided the best thing to do would be to find a place to sleep and lie low until night when he could move more easily. But finding a suitable resting place was not without its difficulties. The country around Crefeld was flat and afforded little cover. He searched as best he could for a hiding place, passing groups of prisoners in the fields and fighting off his natural instinct to run for it whenever he saw a prison guard. Finally, he found a small copse and exhausted almost to the point of dropping he staggered into it and lay down. Although there were some farm workers labouring in the fields nearby, he was too worn out to care about them and fell into a deep sleep.

The sound of a barking dog woke Evans with a start. The animal darted into the copse, through the undergrowth, but luckily it paid no attention to him and went off in search for rabbits. Not long after, a young girl and a man passed through the copse not far from where Evans lay and came within feet of discovering him. It was a close thing but they too made off without spotting the fugitive.

When night came, Evans left the cover of the copse and struck out across the fields. He walked throughout the night using his compass to guide him until dawn the following morning, when he found a cosy hide to lie-up in for a while. He didn't wait for long and just after 6 a.m. he began to walk again, this time tramping right through a village. He had no sooner reached open country again when he was overcome by utter exhaustion once more. He slid into some thick bushes at the top of a gravel pit and collapsed into sleep. Evans lay there until noon before he woke with his throat burning. It was a boiling-hot day and he had very little water left in his water bottle so, throwing caution to the winds, he went off in search of some. This was a mistake for at one point as he emerged from a patch of woods, he was seen by a man who for a moment looked as if he might be suspicious of Evans but he showed no sign of it and Evans casually wandered back into the woods. There were no shouts or cries of alarm from the man so Evans felt he had aroused no suspicion and returned to his hiding place where he fell into a sleep once more. The near encounter with the man was, however, a sharp lesson to him. Wandering about in the open country was inviting trouble so he stayed in hiding until night.

It must have been nine o'clock in the evening when Evans finally decided it was safe to begin walking again. He figured out that he was by then about ten miles from the frontier but according to his map the route he intended taking was barred by villages and he would have to walk a good fifteen miles to skirt round them.

Evans made off through the night desperately thirsty

but managed to stave off his craving for water by chewing the roots of plants. On he went, partially refreshed by the succulent roots but he must have mis-read his compass at one point for he discovered he was walking in quite the wrong direction. The night was quiet and peaceful and he saw no one but he was furious with himself for losing his way. He had hoped to make an attempt on the border that night but his wide detour had cost him valuable time. At last the contours of the country changed and he came to difficult ground, wild and heavily forested with thick woods of pine which made the going difficult. To make matters worse, the country was hilly and his progress slowed up almost to a crawl. But he had, he figured, reached the border area and he lay down to rest amongst some heather. He woke at dawn and decided, by consulting his map, that he was no more than a mile from the frontier.

Evans was only too aware that making a bid to cross the frontier in daylight would be disastrous. He would have to try at night. But in order to make the crossing as easy as possible, he decided to spy out the land during the day to discover the best route to cross. If what he had been told back at the camp about the frontier defences was true, he had a formidable obstacle ahead of him and crossing blindly at night would be courting disaster.

There were wide avenues of grass which divided the dense forest into neat areas of trees and Evans was fairly sure that these open spaces would be patrolled by border guards. He couldn't possibly make his way through the trees, firstly because they were too dense and secondly because the noise he would make would be bound to raise a sentry. He would, he realised, have to creep along the edge of the avenues. He slipped out from the cover of the wood and gingerly made his way along one of the avenues. Keeping well into the edge, he continued like this for almost three hours before stopping and slipping into the young trees by the edge of the avenue. There, he ate some more food and rested. The border must be near now, he reasoned, and he noticed a well worn path running down the avenue. He hadn't been there long when a German frontier guard walked down the path wheeling a bicycle. The German did not see him and he knew then that he hadn't far to go. When the guard was out of sight Evans crawled out into the spacious avenue and had a good look round. Over the tops of some trees at the end of the gap he could just make out the roof of a house with a flag-pole. He was closer to the frontier than he had first thought. It was then that he caught a glimpse of a man by the edge of the woods near the house. He had a rifle slung over his shoulder.

Somehow, Evans determined, he would have to get a better view of the frontier post to assess its exact position in relation to the frontier so he crawled through the woods, crossing yet another ride then striking west towards the frontier through a wide expanse of heather and young trees. He struggled through it then peered over the top of it, finding himself only twenty-five yards or so from a hut with a German sentry standing outside it. He scrambled into some long grass and froze lying half in and half out of it. But just then he heard a noise nearby. He moved his head just far enough to see there was another German, this one unarmed, walking casually along a path which passed within a few feet of where Evans lay. He dared not move. The slightest rustle would alert the German and he lay riveted to the spot, hardly daring to breathe as the man drew closer. His feet were protruding from the grass and through the tall blades he could see the soldier wandering towards him. Then the German's eyes fell on the legs protruding from the grass. He'd been spotted. There was no chance of escape so Evans rose from the grass.

'Who the devil are you?' asked the startled German.

Evans paused for a moment, desperately searching his mind for a plausible story but what came out was a weak one.

'I'm a papermaker from Darmstadt. I'm on a walking holiday, you see and I lost my way in the woods. I was just having a lie down for a bit of a rest.'

'You were, were you?' the German said suspiciously. 'You'll have papers then to prove who you are?'

'Er, yes, of course I have,' Evans replied, hoping that he would get off with not having to show them but even he knew that he hadn't a hope.

'Well, you'd better come with me to the sentry post and we'll have a look at these papers of yours. Come on!'

Evans pretended he'd not heard what the German said and asked:

'I'm nowhere near the frontier, am I?'

'Never mind where you are. That's none of your business. You'll soon find out when you've proved your identity. Now come along and make it fast or I'll call out the guard.'

Evans knew that he'd been caught good and proper and it seemed there was no way out. If he tried to make a dash for it, he would be gunned down by the sentry outside the hut. He had no alternative but to do as he was told and he followed the German along the path towards the hut. But then a chance of escape presented itself. To reach the hut, they had to follow the path into a deepish pit which obscured them from the view of the sentry. Evans acted quickly. He bolted away from the German and into some sparse woods with the sentry hot on his heels and yelling blue murder at him.

Evans charged on through the woods then veered off at an angle but the sentry was with him. His lungs were pounding in his chest as he thrust on through the trees and undergrowth then he emerged on to a road and was instantly confronted by another German levelling a rifle at him. A cry echoed through the forest from the man ...

'Halt!'

Evans, not wishing to take the full force of a bullet fired at almost point blank range, slid to a stop. He was 'in the bag' once more. Soon he was surrounded by Germans, some of them leading dogs, who seemed to appear as if from nowhere. The woods had been crawling with them and it was something of a miracle that he had not been caught earlier.

Crestfallen and angry with himself for taking a chance and venturing from his hide in daylight he was led off to the sentry post along the road. There he was unceremoniously shoved inside and ordered to sit. The German who had pursued him through the woods pointed out to him in no uncertain terms that if he tried to escape again he would be shot dead. However, after having recovered from his initial annoyance at having been 'led a dance' through the woods, the German's anger subsided and he proved to be a kindly sort and gave Evans a welcome cup of tea and a cigarette.

Evans drank the tea thankfully. It was the first hot drink he'd had for some time, and he drew heavily on the cigarette. When he finally stubbed the butt out in an ashtray, the guards got to work on him, searching him thoroughly and taking away his compass and map but they left him with his other bits and pieces. It was pretty obvious that he was no papermaker from Darmstadt and realising that the game was well and truly up, Evans explained to the guards that he was an English flier who had escaped from a prisoner-of-war camp. At this they were delighted. To capture such a prize was quite a feather in their caps. These were not the hard-bitten German soldiers who were to be found at the front. They were generally older men who, because of their age or some infirmity, were not suitable for action and in a way they felt rather sorry for the Englishman. After all he had come within only *twenty yards* of freedom.

Evans sat in the chair waiting for something to be done about him and looking out of the window towards the Dutch border. He was disheartened at having got so near to the border and not making it. The guards eventually went out of the room leaving only an older man with Evans and a sentry outside the door. Evans pretended to sleep but in fact was very much awake, waiting for a chance to 'jump' the old man. If he ran fast enough, he thought, he could take the Germans by surprise and be over the Dutch border before they realised what he was about.

The old man who stood by the door kept a careful watch on his charge but as time dragged on and two hours had elapsed, his concentration began to wane. Now was the time to strike.

Evans leapt up from his chair and hurtled himself at the man, bowling him over on to the floor then he scrambled to his feet and darted outside, crashing into the sentry. But Evans didn't get more than a few yards before he was pounced upon by four or five others who knocked him to the ground and bundled on top of him, crushing him under their accumulated weight. They punched and kicked him then one drew a bayonet and lashed out at the prostrate Evans, cutting him on the head with its sharp point. Blood poured from his wound, covering his face as he lay on the ground unable to defend himself against the fists that continued to thud into his body. At last, when they were satisfied that he could no longer resist, the guards one by one drew back from him and he was hauled to his feet, battered and bruised with blood covering his clothes. After his pummelling, he was in no real condition to walk but the guards insisted he march and he was forced down the road to the neighbouring village of Brüggen, where he was interrogated by an officer who established who Evans was and where he had come from.

At length, Evans was escorted back to Clausthal where he was placed in solitary confinement and after a few days, Kicq was put in with him to share his cell and work out their punishment together. The arrival of his fellow escaper made life in the punishment cell more bearable for Evans. Indeed it was hardly punishment at all since the two men found plenty to occupy their time. Kicq gave Evans Spanish lessons, while Evans tried to brush up Kicq's English. Otherwise they spent their time reading or scheming how they could make another escape attempt.

During their confinement, one of the sentries told Evans that rumour had it he had actually been across the border when he was arrested. The frontier it seemed was not clearly defined at that point and he had wandered over it into no man's land and had been captured there. Evans never did find out whether or not this was true, but it was a most unsettling theory for him to contemplate.

In the latter days of their close confinement, Evans and Kicq learned that they were to be transferred to another camp, one they had heard of but about which they knew nothing. It was at Ingolstadt and after they had worked out their punishment sentence, they were escorted under heavy guard to a train which was to take them there. The journey was long and uncomfortable and during its entirety there was no chance of escape. They arrived in Ingolstadt at mid-day and were led under escort to the prisoner-of-war camp. The sight that confronted them was far from heartening.

The town of Ingolstadt had in those days a population of around 40,000 and stretched over both banks of the Danube. The prisoner-of-war camp was specially reserved for the 'bad boys', the habitual escapers. It consisted of several old forts which had been converted for the purpose and Evans and Kicq were assigned to Fort 9, the top security fort for 'extra-special' prisoners. The countryside around Fort 9 could not have been less promising for the prisoner with escape in mind. It was flat with little or no cover at all and indeed the whole area was extremely dull and uninteresting.

The fort itself consisted of a huge oblong mound about 350 yards long and 60-odd feet high, covered with grass with a wide moat surrounding it. The moat, Evans later discovered, was about 6 feet deep in the middle. Surrounding this was a low wall which obscured most of the fort from the outside.

Evans and Kicq were led to a huge iron gate in the wall which creaked open and they were pushed in. A narrow road led over the moat into a courtyard in front of the massive mound of grass which covered the fort. It was only then that they noticed the barred windows at intervals along the length of the mound. The prisoners' quarters were in fact underground, a thought which pleased neither man since escape would inevitably prove more difficult.

When they entered the courtyard they found it crammed with prisoners of all nationalities but predominantly Russian, French and British. They had arrived in the middle of *appel* (roll-call) but the scene that presented itself to the two men resembled more a football crowd milling into Wembley on cup-final day. There appeared to be no system whatsoever and the prisoners seemed hell-bent on frustrating every attempt the Germans made to count them. It was a veritable shambles and amid the seething mass of humans stood a podgy German captain, red in the face with anger and waving his arms in the air, shouting hell and damnation at the prisoners. The frustrated German was none other than the camp commandant, who was invariably the butt of much invective from the prisoners, notably the French, who took infinite delight in storming into his office at the least provocation and protesting at their lot in a way in which only the French are masters.

Evans and Kicq got a taste of the French attitude when they were led through the milling crowd of prisoners and into the reception bureau. After a short wait the commandant came in but he was closely pursued by a pack of Frenchmen gesticulating madly and protesting as vehemently as they could about having to stand so long in the cold during *appel*. The commandant, already near breaking point, turned on them, threatening to have them shot, but the prisoners, secure in the knowledge that he could do no such thing as it would cause a riot, continued having their fun. Totally exasperated, the commandant summoned the guard but rather than give the commandant the satisfaction of seeing them herded out at rifle point, the Frenchmen left in an orderly fashion.

The diminutive commandant, at his wit's end, heaved a sigh of relief and turned to the two men who had been waiting patiently witnessing the fun. Mopping his brow, he formally 'welcomed' them to Fort 9, a camp which, he assured them, was escape-proof. He went to great lengths to point out that any attempt to escape would result in the severest punishment and that all the guards had orders to shoot to kill if they sighted a prisoner making an escape attempt.

Both Evans and Kicq had heard it all before but rather than antagonise the commandant at so early a stage in their stay, they heard him out in silence and were then led off by guards to their quarters under the grass-covered mound. Both men were shown into a small but adequate room which already housed four officer prisoners, some of whom Evans already knew. They were Grinnell-Milne, Fairweather, Oliphant and Medlicott, all four of whom soon put the two newcomers into the picture about the set-up in the camp.

It seemed, they were told, that almost every prisoner in the fort had either tried to escape or was currently working on some escape plot. Few if any of them indulged in the normal recreations of prisoners of war, like games or studies. They were much too busy planning how to get out of the place. There were amongst the prisoners men who had become specialists in almost every conceivable art likely to aid the escaper. Artists whose skilled hands could bring life to a blank piece of canvas turned their talents to forging documents while others became highly skilled with needle and thread and could transform a uniform into a presentable suit of civilian clothes. A home-made camera was secreted somewhere in the camp and used to photograph would-be escapers for *ausweis* (identity card) photographs. Other prisoners manufactured maps of specific areas in Germany. In fact Fort 9 was nothing less than a factory churning out the goods necessary for escape. Lectures were held in secret where an experienced escaper would give talks, passing on to other prisoners his experiences outside the wire. Throughout the camp there was a tremendous sense of camaraderie and willingness to help each other in whatever way they could to pull off an escape.

Contrary to what the commandant had claimed about the camp being escape-proof, many prisoners had got away from Fort 9 but their greatest problem had come outside the wire. Most of them had been caught either before they reached a frontier or in the process of trying to get across one.

Some of the means of escape used by the prisoners were comic in the extreme. One brave fellow overcame the first obstacle, the moat, by painting his face green and swimming across face up, fooling the guards into thinking that his face was a water lily! Others had escaped in rubbish baskets or by posing as German officers and walking boldly out of the front gate. The ground under the fort was a veritable warren of tunnels, most of them half finished. The moat proved to be an insuperable barrier for the tunnellers and none had actually succeeded in escaping by that means.

Evans and Kicq were greatly heartened by the news of the escape activity in the camp. Immediately upon their arrival, they joined the Room 45 Escaping Club where all of them would pool their resources to effect a breakout.

There was one major problem which faced them. If they were to make any sort of escape attempt at night they had to find out just how many sentries were on watch during the hours of darkness, where they were positioned and their movements. They were confined to their rooms after dark and, since there was only one window in their room and it allowed them a view of only a limited area, they could not watch the sentries properly and chart their routes. Somehow one of them would have to hide outside the mound overnight and get the information they wanted. The six of them put their heads together and one of them hit on an idea. Under the pretence of gardening, they would dig a shallow 'grave' with a false top to it and the 'spy' would get into this grave and carry out his reconnaissance from there during the night, staying there until morning when he would be let out by the other prisoners. On the face of it the idea seemed sound but there was yet another problem. A count of heads was made by the Germans just before lights out when all the doors of the fort were secured. The count was carried out by one German n.c.o. who moved from one room to the next counting the occupants as he went. It was clear that he would notice a man was missing from room 45 if a plan were not devised to fool him into believing that all was well. After a deal of thought, they came up with a scheme. They removed a panel from the wall and so altered it by a skilful bit of carpentry that it could be removed and replaced within seconds and look as if it had not been touched. With the co-operation of the men in the room next to theirs they planned things so that when the guard had counted the men in room 44 and was moving on to room 45, one of the men from 44 would dash through the hole in the wall and into 45, taking the place of the missing man who was in the grave. Luckily the Germans merely counted heads in the rooms and took little notice of identities of the occupants. To the utter amazement of the Room 45 Escape Committee, the scheme actually worked on several occasions and after all of them had taken turns of spending a freezing night in the 'grave' they had a complete breakdown of the sentry system on the camp.

But winter was setting in with a vengeance and the camp was held in the grip of it. This was not a good time for escape. Survival during a trek to the frontier would be made more hazardous than ever in the freezing conditions but it did have one advantage—the moat quickly froze over and this made crossing it very much easier. More than one break-out was made by dashing across the ice and Kicq was among those who tried but none of them was successful and, although Evans was tempted to have a crack at it that way, he persuaded himself not to. His principal reason was that after a recent rush of escapes the Bavarian guards had been given strict orders to shoot to kill and this time the commandant meant what he said. More than one of the escapers who tried their luck over the moat had narrowly escaped death. They had been saved only by the fact that the sentries' hands were freezing cold and they were unable to aim accurately.

The days dragged by wearily for Evans and he fast

became impatient and determined to try an escape over the ice—bullets or no bullets. His plan was simple. He would wait until the last *appel* of the day before making his move. After the roll had been called, he would, under cover of darkness, make a dash for it down the slope that led to the moat and across the ice, over the perimeter wall which was quite low and out into the country. The moat was some 40 yards across and it would be quite a run over the slippery ice with the sentries firing at him but he was so frustrated at being cooped up in the camp that he was determined to risk almost anything to make good his escape. The trigger-happy sentries were by no means the only hazard he would have to face in his bolt for freedom; there was the ice itself. The question was posed—'Would it hold?' Evans tested it by casually throwing heavy stones on to it. It seemed to be strong enough but there was no way of testing it under the weight of a man. That, however, was a chance he would have to take.

Kicq and another prisoner called Wilkin agreed to accompany Evans on his dash for freedom and one day when the *appel* bell rang their plan swung into operation. Each of them carrying his pack of goods and provisions made a bolt for it down the slope with Evans well in the lead. He fairly leapt on to the ice and, praising the Almighty when he landed, it held and he dashed on.

Evans had gone about half way before he heard the first cry of 'Halt' and the shots began to ring out with bullets chipping into the ice by his feet. He struggled on, though the going was hard, and he scrambled on to the far bank, glancing back to catch sight of his comrades. They unfortunately had not met with the same luck as he had. Both of them trod gingerly on to the edge of the ice but in doing so had gone right through it because the ice at the edge was thin and weak. Both of them had to struggle on to the harder stuff under a hail of fire from the sentries. Luckily the guards' aim was far from accurate and they missed by some distance.

Kicq and Wilkin made it to the other side and were hot on the heels of Evans who dashed across the snow, over the low wall and into a field. He had no sooner done so than he saw in front of him a group of sturdy German farm workers. They had witnessed his escape and were dashing towards him, one of them brandishing a whip.

Weak with exertion but determined not to let them get him Evans dashed away from them but even then guards were pouring out of the fort. The man with the whip was the first to catch up with Evans and he lashed out at him with it, catching him across the back and the neck. The pain stung him and he paused for a moment. In that fraction of a second the others were on top of him and he was recaptured. Both Kicq and Wilkin were rounded up by the guards and all three men were taken back again to their cage. Each of them was sentenced to solitary confinement but as the cells were so crowded with other prisoners serving their sentences for escape attempts and minor offences, the three of them were merely put on the waiting list which meant that they would serve their sentences when cells became vacant. Evans and the others determined that they would not be around when their turn came and they set about planning another escape.

Life in the fort was becoming progressively worse as the weather grew colder. It seemed impossible to keep warm and the solitary stove in room 45 gave off little heat even when the occupants supplemented the meagre ration of coal with wood stolen from all over the fort. They stole every piece of wood they could lay their hands on and became so adept at it that the Germans issued an order indicating that anyone caught stealing wood would be shot on sight.

It was Christmas time when Evans and the others came

to hear of an escape plot being hatched by a group of Frenchmen. They had been hard at work sawing through the iron bars which covered a window in the latrines. It was, they thought, an ideal exit point since the sentry who patrolled outside it had a forty-yard 'beat' and if the break-out could be made when he was at the far end of his beat he would have little chance of catching the escapers. The job of cutting through the bar was a tiring one and Evans and Medlicott offered their services in return for the chance of escape with the Frenchmen. They agreed and they were in on the plan.

The work on the bars went slowly because the slightest noise might alert the sentry but progress it did and finally all was set for the great escape. Evans and Medlicott had all their kit prepared for the break-out but on the very day they intended to go, the commandant and a *feldwebel* (sergeant) discovered that the bars had been tampered with. They must have been tipped-off for the cuts in the bars were so well disguised that they could not have been spotted by a casual glance. Someone, they never discovered who, had turned traitor and had given the game away. They had their suspicions of one of the French prisoners but could not prove anything.

As a result of the discovery, the commandant ordered that a barbed wire entanglement be placed over the hole and an additional sentry stationed there to keep watch on it. It seemed that their scheme had been foiled completely and the French gave up the idea. But one night as he stood in the latrines 'minding his own business', Evans took a closer look at the wire over the window and at the sentry outside. Perhaps, he thought, this wasn't quite as difficult as it looked. The barbed wire entanglement was not deep—and could be cut.

Without hesitation, he dashed into room 45 and roused Medlicott and Wilkin who followed him to the latrines, bringing a pair of wire-cutters Wilkin had with them.

Gingerly, Wilkin cut one of the wires. The resulting noise seemed to echo throughout the fort but the sentry who paced his beat outside took no notice. They cut more strands of wire and still the sentry paid no attention. Soon they had cut quite a sizeable hole with enough room for them to get through. On the spur of the moment, they decided there and then to make a break for it.

Wilkin, who had not lately been in the best of health, decided against throwing in his lot with Evans and Medlicott. He sensibly decided to wait until he was fit again before making an attempt at escape. That left only Evans and Medlicott to make the break but they had to work fast if they were to pull it off. They hurried back to room 45 and stuffed their escape equipment into rucksacks and donned their civilian clothing before returning to the latrines.

Medlicott tossed a coin to decide who should go first and he won. While Wilkin kept a lookout for the sentry, Medlicott eased back the cut strands of wire until a hole had been made. Then Wilkin gave the signal. The sentry was at the far end of his beat. Now was the time to go. Medlicott struggled into the hole in the wire but was immediately stuck fast and the sentry had turned and was coming back. Both Evans and Wilkin hauled him back. He had too much clothing on to get through the hole and was obliged to discard some of it. The sentry passed by the window and carried on his beat, failing to notice the gap in the wire in the darkness. Again Medlicott scrambled through the hole and this time he made it, followed closely by Evans. They dashed with all their might down the slope to the moat and on to the ice. They ran like madmen over the slippery surface as the first staccato yells came from the guard:

'Halt! Halt!'

As they lunged at the far bank of the moat, a shot rang out but it was wide of the mark and bit into the bank a few yards ahead of them. They shinned over the wall and darted into some young trees as the sentries fired blindly at them. Evans and Medlicott sped through the small trees brushing the branches aside with their flailing arms until they emerged into open fields. There they struck off to the north but already they could see moving lights behind them. The guard was out and in hot pursuit.

With hearts and heads pounding, they dashed on over the fields until they reached another wood which they leapt into. By then the guards were no more than 300 yards behind them. The trees were sparse and there was no undergrowth in which to hide. Recapture was at hand if they could not find a way of throwing them off the scent. They crouched for a moment in the trees watching the lights which were spread out in a line approaching them. There was one large gap in the lights and they determined to make a dash for it through the gap. The sentries would not expect them to back-track.

Half bent, they scurried through the gap coming at one point within 20 yards of the sentries and made off towards the village. Once there they chose a road which led off to the south and they marched boldly down it, trudging through the deep snow. There was not a soul to be seen but when they reached a house and were just about to pass it, they heard a faint noise from a clump of trees. There was someone there. As one they shot off into a field but as they did so a man emerged from the trees. He saw them and yelled to them to halt.

Evans glanced back and in the moonlight saw that the man was a soldier with his arm extended towards them. His hand was clutching a pistol and the business end of it was pointing their way. It was no good; they'd been caught once more and they'd no hope of making it through the snow. The German could easily gun them down. They stood rigidly still, lest the man should think they were going to bolt for it and shoot. When he came close to them they recognised him as one of the corporals from the camp. Luckily for them he was one of the few decent ones with whom they were on reasonably friendly terms otherwise their fate might have been quite different.

The corporal marched them back to the camp but as they entered the main gate they found a posse of guards waiting for them and their mood was decidedly ugly. The wrath of the commandant would descend upon them later when he discovered that the two men had been allowed to escape from the camp and they were in hot water. One of them lunged forward at the two Englishmen brandishing a bayonet and threatening to disembowel them there and then but the corporal intervened. Had the corporal not been there they would certainly have been beaten up or worse.

At that a burly sergeant arrived and cursed the corporal for bringing them back alive. He had a murderous look in his eyes and Evans knew that given the chance, the sergeant would cheerfully have shot both of them on the spot. After a tongue-lashing from him they were marched off back into the camp, where the commandant sentenced them to several days solitary for the escape attempt, a fairly mild punishment considering the tense atmosphere in the camp.

As the months dragged on, conditions in the camp grew steadily worse. Security was tightened and the few privileges the prisoners had were withdrawn as more and more escape attempts were made. Riots on a fairly minor scale became commonplace in the fort and the guards became trigger-happy, blasting off at anything that looked remotely suspicious. At last the situation reached such a state that the authorities decided to move the British and Russian prisoners to another camp, leaving the troublesome French where they were so that they could be dealt with more effectively.

Evans discovered that they were to be sent to a camp at Zorndorf, which lay a considerable distance from Ingolstadt. A fellow prisoner, called Buckley, who had been in captivity at Zorndorf before coming to Ingolstadt, told him that it was one of the worst camps in Germany. The conditions there, he informed Evans, were infinitely worse than those at Fort 9 and Evans determined that one way or another, he would make a break for it before reaching the new camp.

Evans and Buckley agreed to team up in an escape attempt and since they were to be leaving the camp in a couple of days there was insufficient time to plan a break from there. They would have to make their escape from the train and it was imperative that they did it as soon as possible since the train would be taking them in the opposite direction to the Swiss border.

The day came for their transportation to the other camp and they were duly marched off to the station where they were herded on to a train. Buckley and Evans found themselves in a compartment with a group of other English prisoners and one guard. The chances of getting out of the compartment seemed slim and clutching their escape rucksacks they sat next to the window which they had been instructed must be kept closed at all times. After a hurried consultation they agreed that the window would be the only way out and at some point they would have to make a jump for it.

The train thundered on until it reached Nuremberg and after a long stop there it pulled out of the station and into the night. It travelled through thickly wooded country, ideal for the escaper, and since the guard understood no English the two would-be escapers discussed with the others in the compartment their plans to make a jump for freedom. All readily agreed to help in any way they could and a plan was conceived and put into operation.

At a point almost 10 miles outside Nuremberg, the train slowed on a steep gradient. The time was right for escape. Evans asked the guard if they might all eat some of the provisions they had packed in their cases and haversacks. The guard agreed and as one the occupants of the carriage rose from their seats to take their cases from the racks above their heads. The compartment was crammed with men and for a few moments the sentry's view of the two men by the window was obscured. In a moment, the window was open and Evans and Buckley dived out to land with a thud on the grass verge. They lay there winded for a few moments, gathering their senses and watching as the train chugged off along the track and eventually out of sight.

There was no hint of the train stopping and both men congratulated each other on their success but with that over they contemplated the march that lay ahead of them. They were some 200 miles from the Swiss border and not well supplied with food for a marathon trek. The prospect of such a walk did not fill them with enthusiasm but at least they were free and, come what may, they were going to have a damn good try for the frontier. Above all, they decided, they would steer clear of habitation in daytime unless they had absolutely no alternative. They would walk by night and hide-up by day. Luckily they both had compasses and, using these to point the way, they set off . . .

The first two nights of their trek passed without incident and they made reasonable progress through the heavily forested country, catching sight of the occasional isolated house on their way. It seemed that every house in Germany had a dog which barked incessantly when they approached. Evans soon built up an acute dislike for the four-legged animals and cursed every one that snapped at them when they passed a house.

On the third night, they stumbled upon a man carrying a gun who eyed them suspiciously but they boldly bade him a good evening and continued on their way. But close shaves like that began to play on their nerves and they soon found that the slightest little idiosyncrasy the other had was bound to result in frayed tempers. By then Evans' feet were blistered badly and were extremely painful. He found walking difficult and the continuous pain did little to help subdue the mounting tension but he stumbled resolutely on trying as best he could to keep up with Buckley.

The fourth night came and went without event but the following night they both got the scare of their lives. It was a Sunday night and they had just passed a village and were resting in a wood on the outskirts when suddenly both of them heard a whistle coming from deeper in the woods. Then there was another, off in the opposite direction. That was followed by more whistling. The woods seemed alive with people all whistling as if signalling to each other. It could be only one thing, they thought—a search-party combing the woods and gradually closing in for the capture.

Moments later there was a rustle in the trees near the road which they had just left. They watched intently to catch sight of what was about to emerge and soon it came. One figure then another and another, crouching low and darting across the road into the woods on the other side. The two fugitives discovered that the mysterious whistling came from boy scouts out on a night exercise. Neither man knew whether to laugh or be angry but they knew they could not wait there any longer. Discovery by the scouts would inevitably have lead to a search-party out hunting for them.

Evans and Buckley got underway again and eventually reached a railway line which they followed and which led them to a good road. This made the going somewhat easier and they progressed well until they came to a signpost, the first they had seen. It pointed to Gunzenhausen. To their delight they found that they were heading in the right direction. Evans' map had not covered the area over which they had just trekked and he was, therefore, relieved to find that they had reached a place which he could identify and pin-point on his map.

With renewed heart they plodded on and invigorated by their discovery, Evans' feet seemed less painful. Then, on the seventh day, they were discovered by an old woman who was collecting sticks from the edge of the wood in which they lay. They bluffed their way through this by using the old tale about being walkers on a tour and this seemed to satisfy the old lady but when she had gone they quickly got under way once more fearing that she might raise the alarm. But they were not followed.

On the eighth night of their walk they got hopelessly lost and found themselves back-tracking and covering ground they had already been over. They had just crossed a bridge and walked about a quarter of a mile when they discovered they had taken the wrong road. They retraced their steps and recrossed the bridge, then studied the map more closely finding to their frustration that they had been on the right road in the first place. Again they crossed the bridge, both cursing each other for their stupidity. This sort of thing happened often and invariably led to arguments and claims that it was the other's fault. The strain of utter physical exhaustion coupled with the ever present nervous tension was telling on them. Furthermore Evans was again in agony with his badly blistered and swollen feet and at times he was in such pain that he just could not walk. Their progress slowed considerably.

On the following night there occurred an incident which puzzled both of them—and gave them a nasty shock as well. They stumbled upon a group of sheds, surrounded by a high barbed-wire fence and powerful arc lights. This place had all the looks of a prisoner-of-war camp and they hastily decided to get as far away from it as possible but then as they did so, they caught sight of a man coming in their direction. From the distance they could see that he was stalking them or somebody else. He was in a crouched posture and carrying a rifle. Neither man hesitated and they scurried off with all speed. They had not gone far, however, when a thick mist descended but with the aid of their compasses they held their course and slid on through the swirling blanket of mist until they reached a railway line. They were about to cross it when two men emerged from the woods on the other side. They took one glance at the two Englishmen and ran for their lives. Evans and Buckley considered what had happened for some time and concluded that they had, by some fantastic coincidence, encountered two more fugitives on the run.

As they trudged on the lack of food became their greatest problem. They had long before run out of their supplies and had taken to stealing potatoes from fields and eating them raw. This helped in some small measure to sustain them but they grew progressively weaker and this resulted in them making foolish mistakes. Time and again they took wrong turnings only to find themselves way off their proper course or at a dead end but they stumbled on as best they could until, on the fourteenth night of their trek, they caught their first glimpse of the mountains of Switzerland. They were close but there still lay dangers ahead. The nearer they got to the frontier the more vigilant the German population would be in hunting down strangers and escapers.

The following evening they passed through some farm land and saw several gangs of Russian prisoners at work on the fields, all under heavy guard. Knowing that there must be a camp nearby they changed course to make a wide detour of the area.

On the eighteenth night of their journey, weary and dishevelled and on the point of complete exhaustion, they reached the village of Riedheim close to the German/Swiss frontier. They had been on the go for eighteen nights and at last they had almost reached their goal. On the outside of the village ran a small stream on the other side of which lay the frontier. From a vantage point above the village they saw the Swiss Alpine Clubhouse which was the frontier post. They were now only half a mile from freedom but they had yet to cross the all important stream and make the 500-yard dash to the frontier post.

Evans and Buckley hid up in the woods all day planning how best to cross to the frontier. From their vantage point they had a good view of the border and could see the sentries posted along it. Getting across it would be difficult but above all they had to avoid discovery before they even tried. The woods were patrolled during the day and at four o'clock in the afternoon a frontier guard plodded through the trees and narrowly missed walking into the two men crouched in the undergrowth.

At 10.15 that night they started off on the last lap of their journey. As they made their way towards the stream, Evans could not help thinking about his previous escapade at the Dutch frontier and how unlucky he had been.

The moon slid behind a cloud and they scrambled to a roadside where they waited, listening for the slightest sound that would betray the presence of a sentry. But no sound came and they bolted across it, then over a railway line and into a water-meadow. The meadow was covered with long, thick grass and they crawled through it but it seemed that their movements echoed across the countryside. Surely they must be discovered, they thought. They slipped into ditches which cut across the meadow and paused for moments to listen. Not a sound, except the faint rustling of the grass in the wind and the murmur of water in the stream.

They slipped across another road which was patrolled but they roused no one, then after crawling on their bellies for some yards they saw the stream ahead of them. Both men stopped for a few seconds, making a final check before moving on. Then they spotted him—a sentry walking along the path which skirted the stream. He looked as if he was just coming off duty. He had no rifle but he had to pass within a few yards of them. They prepared themselves to fight it out if they were discovered but lay motionless in the grass as the sentry drew closer. They were poised, ready to battle for all their worth but the sentry merely sauntered past them.

When the German had disappeared out of sight, the men heaved a sigh of relief. It was now or never. Crouching they dashed to the stream and in a few bounds were across it and on to the opposite bank. They bolted like men possessed across the ground until they reached a rough road. They followed this for a few minutes until they came to a large notice-board which proclaimed that the ground beyond it was Switzerland. They paused for a moment, drinking in the reality of what they had achieved and hardly able to believe what they had done, then together they stepped across the border. They were free.

Evans, one of the most determined escapers of the First World War, had more than earned his freedom. They had crossed the frontier just after midnight on 9 June, 1917, and had been in captivity for more than a year. After the formalities had been gone through and they had both eaten and drunk their fill for several days, they made their way back to Britain.

Evans was soon back in action but this time in a different clime in the near east. It seemed, however, that the intrepid escaper was destined to be a prisoner. In February, 1918, Evans was commanding a bomber squadron in Palestine when he was captured by the Turks. This time he did not escape and after a few months in prison was repatriated when the war ended. During the Second World War, he put his experiences to good use, instructing servicemen in the art of escape and of evading capture. Many would-be escapers of that war were to be grateful for the wisdom of A. J. Evans and indeed it was through reading his book *The Escaping Club** that many of them were inspired to escape at all.

* Published in 1921 by Jonathan Cape

# 2

# *The Shepherd of Hydekrug*

It seems that, in spite of all the Germans had learned of keeping Allied prisoners 'behind the wire' during the First World War, there was no fully escape-proof prisoner-of-war camp in the second major conflict of the century—not even the notorious Colditz Castle, which housed 'special' prisoners. Every camp, whether it was in Germany itself or in German-occupied territory, had its quota of escapes. Most of these escape attempts resulted in recapture but some men got through and returned to Britain to take up arms once more.

Some camps were more difficult to escape from than others, partially because of the efficiency of their commandants and on the other hand because of their geographical location. Breaking out of the camp itself was a big enough problem for the would-be escaper but he inevitably faced his greatest test when, in many cases, he was faced with a trek over hundreds of miles through hostile country with no hope of help from anyone 'on the outside'. If the fugitive were fortunate enough to reach France, then he at least had the advantage of a helping hand from the Underground to shepherd him through German-occupied territory to neutral ground or to the coast where he could be picked up by a British ship or submarine. There was no effective Underground system in Germany which the escaper could call upon for help and it was invariably during the first few days, while still in Germany, that escapers were caught.

Once outside the wire, the escaper's sole objective was to reach neutral territory as quickly as possible even if, at the end of the journey, he was faced with the possibility of internment. This at least was preferable to life in a prisoner-of-war camp. If he weren't arrested as an illegal immigrant by the authorities in neutral Sweden, Switzerland or Spain, he was guaranteed help from a British embassy.

In every prisoner-of-war camp, even in the very early stages of the war, groups of prisoners formed themselves into escape committees so that escape attempts could be made on an organised basis. They took it upon themselves to collate information received and to utilise the talents and skills of the prisoners in the manufacture of forged passes, maps, civilian clothes and escape equipment such as keys and saws. They accumulated money with which to bribe guards and built up stores of food and supplies which an escaper could use to survive on. They became the camp intelligence service and the brains behind escape attempts. One of their prime functions was to ensure that no two escape attempts clashed and they kept up a liaison with foreign escape committees to this end.

From the very beginning, escape committees in the camps throughout Germany realised that if their men were to have any hope of success in escaping, some sort of organisation would have to be set up in that country to help them on their way. But the problem was, how? They could not expect the British Secret Service to spare precious agents to set up such an organisation. Trained secret agents were scarce and the few there were, were engaged in the business of building up resistance organisations in the occupied countries. It became clear that there could be only one way of setting up such an organisation and that was for the prisoners to do it themselves. But how could an escape committee seriously expect a prisoner to break out of a camp and remain in Germany to help his fellows? For obvious reasons, every prisoner wanted to get back to Britain to freedom. There was, however, one man willing to undertake the task; a man who put aside his desire for freedom that others might escape. He was warrant officer G.T.W. Grimson, an observer in the Royal Air Force who fell into German hands in 1940 when his bomber was shot down during a raid. But although Grimson became the most persistent R.A.F. escaper of all during the Second World War, he never did succeed in returning to England. Like so many other wartime heroes, he ultimately paid the supreme penalty for his courage ...

Following his capture, Grimson was imprisoned in Stalag Luft 1 at Barth, where, like most 'other ranks' he was put to work. Unlike officer prisoners who, according to the terms of the Geneva Convention, were not obliged to work during imprisonment, Grimson found himself on a working party. The very fact that n.c.o.s were obliged to work gave them the edge on officers as far as escaping was concerned for it afforded them greater opportunities of escape while outside the camp. Quite a few took advantage of this and some of them succeeded.

Grimson, not long after his arrival at Stalag Luft 1 was on one such working party outside the camp when he saw his chance. His guard had his back to him and Grimson, seizing the opportunity, kicked the German hard in the small of the back, knocking him to the ground, then he made a bolt for it. But the guard quickly recovered and summoned others who rounded up Grimson within a few minutes. He was roughly manhandled back to the camp where the commandant had him thrown into the camp gaol for two weeks. Once in solitary confinement he reflected upon his escape bid, realising that he hadn't a hope and that making an attempt on the spur of the moment was almost certainly bound to result in recapture or worse still a bullet in the back as he ran.

The months dragged monotonously on at Barth but while the daily drudgery of camp life continued, Grimson was preparing for his next attempt. This time he resolved not to make the same mistakes he'd made before. 'Impulse' escape bids were out. He realised that an escaping prisoner would stand precious little chance of travelling undetected across Germany without being able to speak the language quite fluently, so he set about learning it from German-speaking prisoners and by conversing with his guards. By 1942, his German was faultless and he began devising a plan of escape. But before he got far in his preparations, he, along with all the other n.c.o.s at Barth, was moved to another camp, Stalag Luft 111* at Sagan, situated some miles south-east of Frankfurt.

Not long after his arrival at this camp, Grimson made his second bid for freedom, but this time he was better prepared. By careful observation he had noticed that there was a striking resemblance between himself and the German corporal who was responsible for the issue of stores. Grimson pondered on how he could use this remarkable coincidence to his advantage and soon came up with a scheme. He 'befriended' the corporal and through bribery and persuasion got the German to lend him his paybook and gate pass. In no time, the expert forgers in the camp had copied the two documents for Grimson before he returned them to the corporal.

Meanwhile, the camp tailors were busily fashioning a

*It was from Stalag Luft 111 that the famous 'Wooden Horse' escape was made in which three Air Force officers escaped to England in October 1943. After a mass escape of Air Force officers through a tunnel from the same camp in 1944, fifty of them were murdered by the Gestapo on Hitler's orders. A memorial now stands at Sagan to the memory of the dead men.

uniform for Grimson. It consisted of a white fatigue jacket made out of towels, an expertly converted field service cap, improvised badges of rank, a leather belt and pistol holster. They did a good job and the likeness when Grimson had a dress rehearsal was staggering.

The time for the break came when the German corporal went on leave. Grimson, clad in the improvised uniform and carrying a bucket full of scrubbing brushes, walked boldly from the equipment store to the main compound gate where the sentry, fooled by the disguise, opened the gate and after a cursory glance at the pass which Grimson proffered let him through. Little did the German realise that beneath the white overalls Grimson wore was a complete civilian outfit and under the scrubbing brushes in the bucket enough supplies of food to keep him alive for some considerable time.

With the first obstacle successfully overcome, Grimson walked on to the next gate outside which was the German compound. He walked between the storehouse and sick quarters which were located in this second compound and came into the view of the gate sentry from that direction, the way in which the sentry would have expected the storeman to come. The second sentry paid little attention to him and did not even bother to speak. He let him through and now Grimson found himself in the German compound. He was then only yards away from open country but it was mid-day and he decided it would be best to lie-up for a while before venturing out of the camp. He dodged into an air-raid shelter and waited there until dark before he sneaked out of the German compound through a gate by the side of the officers' mess. Then he disposed of his uniform. Alas his liberty was short-lived for a few days later he was arrested by police when his documents were checked and they noticed a discrepancy. Back he was brought to Sagan but he was far from dispirited at his lack of success and set about plotting yet another escape. His short spell of freedom had given him a taste for the 'fresh open spaces' and he launched himself into escape plans with determination.

It was some six months later that the opportunity arose once more. The day after Christmas 1942, the prisoners arranged to give a concert to which the German officers were invited. It was while the concert was in progress that Grimson and a fellow prisoner made their escape attempt. Both of them were dressed in the uniforms of German corporals, again supplied by the camp tailors. They walked briskly towards the first of two gates and shouted to the sentry who was some way off to open up. The sentry was a few yards away from the gate at the time but he quickened his pace and came to it. The two 'corporals' flashed their forged passes while they gave the guard a tongue-lashing for taking so long to open the gate. The sentry, not wishing to incur the displeasure of the two n.c.o.s, obliged and they passed through. But they were not to find it quite so easy at the next gate. They approached this one and showed their passes but then the sentry asked them for their entry numbers. They were stumped. No one had warned them that such numbers were required under a new rule recently introduced, but almost without hesitation, Grimson turned on the sentry and demolished him with invective, tearing a strip off him for delaying them. In the confusion, the sentry opened the gate and the two men walked quickly through, muttering oaths at the sentry as they went.

They walked directly through the German compound and out of the same gate Grimson had used before and into some nearby woods where they quickly changed clothes and made off for Sagan railway station, disguised as foreign workers. At the station, they bought tickets and travelled by train to Bayreuth, but again their documents let them down and both of them were arrested and shipped back to Sagan. Grimson's third attempt had failed but he was determined not to give up. Six months later, he tried again …

On this, his fourth escape bid, Grimson used a disguise once more. He was fast becoming a master of the art of disguise with the aid of the many experts on camp. This time he was to pose as a German telephone engineer. From time to time these engineers carried out repairs on the telephone wire which ran along the tops of the compound perimeter fences. Under the watchful eyes of the sentries in the machine-gun towers, the engineers were free to scale the fences on both sides to carry out their repairs. Grimson intended following suit but once over the fence, he would stroll off to freedom. At least that was the plan …

The camp escape committee arranged to supply him with the appropriate uniform which consisted of a boiler suit, a leather belt and a field service cap. They even gave him an imitation electrician's meter together with the required documents and a supply of food.

Then one afternoon, clad in his overalls and carrying a 'borrowed' ladder, he made his way to the perimeter fence and boldly shouted up to the guard in a nearby tower that he was going to test the telephone wires at the top of the fence. The guard nodded and yelled to another in a tower farther along the perimeter fence, indicating that the engineer had permission to enter the strip of ground between a first guard-rail and the double row of fencing. When the all-clear had been given by both guards, Grimson propped his ladder against the fence and climbed up it, then a brilliant piece of play-acting ensued when he began 'testing' the telephone lines with the aid of his dummy meter. But somehow he had to find an excuse to get over the other row of fencing. Luckily the wire at that point stretched across the gap from the inner to the outer fence and he indicated to the guard in the tower that he would have to examine the wire on the other fence. The guard gave him the O.K. and Grimson clambered down the ladder and fetched a long plank of wood which he used as a bridge over the gap. He slid over this and continued 'working' on the wires but he had no sooner done so than the sentry who was patrolling outside the fence stopped and asked him what he was up to. Grimson explained that a fault had been reported and he was putting it right. But the sentry was not altogether satisfied with his explanation and asked to see his papers. Grimson obliged, showing him the false documents which had been specially provided for him. The sentry looked at them, nodded and then returned them and went on his way at which Grimson clambered back up the fence once more. Time was running out, however, and every moment he lingered heightened his chances of his ruse being uncovered, so he decided to act then.

Grimson 'accidentally' dropped his test meter amongst the barbed wire entanglement on the outside of the fence. He shouted to the guard and told him what had happened, then he clambered down the outer fence, adding to the impression of annoyance by cursing volubly in German. He picked up the meter and told the guard that it was broken and he would have to go and get another. The guard nodded and Grimson walked off into the German compound, ostensibly to replace the broken meter. But the telephone engineer did not linger a moment longer than was necessary and walked straight out of the camp and disposed of his uniform before boarding a train, bound for the Baltic port of Stettin.

Grimson duly arrived at Stettin and set about scouring the docks for a neutral ship on which he hoped to stow away but alas his luck was out again and one day, while walking through the docks, he was arrested. He had been at large for five days.

Once more Grimson found himself behind the wire. He was bitterly disappointed. He'd got so close to pulling it off, closer than he had done in any of his other three escapes but he'd been snatched at the last moment. To many this would have been the end of the line. They'd have given up in desperation—but not Grimson. He was hell-bent on having another crack at getting home but before he could, he and many others in Stalag Luft 111 were transferred to Stalag Luft 6 at Hydekrug, in East Prussia, close to the frontier of Lithuania and the wide expanse of the Baltic Sea, across which lay Sweden and possible freedom. The prospect of making a successful escape from this camp and reaching neutral Sweden was infinitely greater than at their previous camp. There were bands of partisans operating nearby and the population of the close-by occupied countries was in the main friendly. With hope renewed, there was a stream of escape bids but all of them ended in failure, due in no small measure to the exhaustion which quickly overcame the weakened prisoners. This fatigue soon led to carelessness which resulted inevitably in capture.

The escape committee soon agreed that the only certain way of ensuring success would be to have a 'hide' somewhere within a reasonable distance of the camp where escapers could lie-up for a while and carefully plan their exit from the country. But to arrange such a thing meant having friends on the outside and being able to contact them. As luck would have it, they found one, a man who subsequently did valiant work for them—and he was a German.

Eddie Munkert was the official German interpreter at Hydekrug. He was a small, thin man who wore thick gold-rimmed glasses—the very antithesis of the Aryan German—but in spite of his somewhat feeble appearance he was a man of immense courage and conviction. Munkert had lived in America for some time before the war then returned to the Fatherland where he joined the Catholic Centre Party. When the Nazis took power this movement was outlawed but Munkert still held resolutely on to his beliefs, hating the Nazis and all they stood for. He could foresee nothing but ultimate doom under the Nazi regime and although outwardly loyal, he determined to do all he could to help bring about their downfall. He was a non-combatant and because of his knowledge of English was subsequently appointed to the job of camp interpreter at Hydekrug where he quickly became a willing helper for the escape organisation. Munkert was in an invaluable position since he could visit the prisoners at any time without rousing suspicion and bring them almost anything they wanted to help in the escape attempts. He smuggled clothing, maps and letters from friends into the camp. He supplied all sorts of vital information which was of immense help to the escape committee.

There was, as well as Munkert, another official in the camp who willingly collaborated with the committee. He was the camp photographer, a Pole called Sommers. Sommers had been a Polish Army officer cadet at the outbreak of the war and was captured by the Russians and in due course handed over to the Germans. Like many of his countrymen, he was given the option of joining the German army or being sent to a labour camp. Sommers had a widowed mother whom he knew could not live without some support from him so he became a naturalised German and was conscripted into the Luftwaffe as a photographer. But in spite of his new-found nationality, Sommers was far from being a loyal German and kept close contact with the Polish Underground Movement. When he was posted to Hydekrug as the camp photographer, he saw his chance of doing his bit for the Allies. He smuggled into the camp vast quantities of photographic material which was used for forging passes and copying maps with which to equip the escapers. Between them, Munkert and Sommers did great work—but their activities were to have tragic consequences.

Not long after Grimson's arrival at Hydekrug, the escape committee got word from the outside by means of a coded letter that there was a Swedish minister doing welfare work for Swedish seamen in one of the Baltic ports. He was, they were told, known to be sympathetic to the prisoners and willing to help and give refuge to escapers. Somehow they had to get in touch with this man and arrange a set-up whereby the escapers could hide-up with him before leaving the country. The committee enlisted the help of Munkert who travelled to several of the Baltic ports searching high and low for the minister but could find no trace of him. But it was about then that another willing helper came to light. He was a guard on the camp and like Sommers was a Pole who had been conscripted. He offered to hide prisoners in his home, a move which had distinct and obvious dangers for the man and his family. The whole thing seemed, on the face of it, just too good to be true but the escape committee checked him out and found that he meant what he said. The Pole's house would be an ideal base from which to work, at least for a time but there was no doubt about it that the committee would have to 'plant' someone there, an organiser who could establish a proper escape route along which prisoners on the run could travel.

Grimson, with his knowledge of German, was the ideal man for the job and he readily agreed to take it on. He would use the Pole's house as a base from which he would operate and scour the Baltic ports to trace the mysterious Swedish minister. This was October 1943 but it was three months before the final preparations had been made and the time was ripe for the escape bid.

Grimson enlisted the aid of yet another Pole who

visited the camp regularly driving a horse-drawn wagon. The driver's seat of this wagon consisted of an upturned box capable of holding a man and the idea was that Grimson would hide in the box and get through the gates in that way. Alas, the plan misfired, for the Pole failed to call at the camp on the appointed day and indeed was not seen again for some time afterwards. It may have been that the man had had second thoughts or been frightened off. Whatever the reason the escape committee had to find another way of getting Grimson out of Stalag Luft 6. A second attempt, disguised as a civilian workman, failed and the escape committee and Grimson got their heads together to devise another means ...

From the escapers' wardrobe, Grimson selected clothes which he hoped would fox the guards. It comprised a civilian outfit, the lower part of which consisted of riding breeches and long boots. Over this he wore a German Air Force greatcoat with crossbelts, an ammunition pouch and a dummy bayonet. The plan was that he would use the daily *appel* as his cover for escape.

On the 21st January, shortly after mid-day, the call for *appel* sounded throughout the camp. It was a freezing-cold day and because of this it was arranged that the head count would be held in the barracks. Before the guards arrived, one of the prisoners took Grimson's place while Grimson, clad in his escape gear, lay in a bed covered by a blanket feigning illness. The count went off without incident and when the guards left, Grimson rose from his 'sick bed' peered out of the barrack window and watched the guards ambling off through the compound gate back to the German compound. As the last few of them went through, he left the barracks and tagged on to the end of the line. The guard on the gate took no notice of him and he walked through.

Once in the German compound he headed for a lavatory where he disposed of a dummy rifle which he'd been carrying then he made his way to a storeroom nearby. The store was locked but Grimson had been supplied with a key which had been made in the camp. He opened the door and once inside found a hidden box which had been planted there previously. It contained his civilian escape clothes. He quickly stripped and donned these clothes then put the German clothes in the box. It had been arranged that these would be removed by Munkert and returned to the escape committee the following day.

Grimson waited in the store for some hours until darkness fell then left, locking it after him and hiding the key in a pre-arranged spot before boldly walking out of the German compound and making his way to the railway station in Hydekrug. He arrived there only minutes before the train was due to leave, bought his ticket and boarded the train. Grimson was at large once more ...

He travelled by train to the city of Danzig, some four hundred miles from Hydekrug, where he made contact with a Polish forester, a friend of the guard at the prisoner-of-war camp. He was greeted warmly and offered all the help he wished. Grimson lost no time in writing a coded message via Munkert to his friends in Hydekrug telling them that he had arrived safely and that he had found an ideal set-up. Above all he needed supplies of tobacco, food and clothing with which to trade with the locals.

The escape committee was delighted with the news and all the supplies Grimson needed were taken to him by a Polish guard who was going on leave to a village near where Grimson was operating. Grimson used the goods he received to good effect, bartering them for information and help which was vital to his operation in the area. But as the days progressed, things began to get too dangerous for Grimson. One of the local women spent too much time talking about Grimson's presence in the house and it seemed it would be only a question of time before the Germans got to know of it. He couldn't take that chance and decided to move out and find another safe hide and also make further attempts to locate the Swedish minister. He passed on this information to the escape committee by way of the Polish guard who was returning to the camp from leave.

The committee was anxious to get some escapes under way and selected a man to make a break. But there was a lull in communication with Grimson for something like two weeks. The committee waited anxiously for news but none came. Then they decided to take a chance and send a letter via Munkert to a postal pick-up point informing Grimson that the other escaper, Warrant Officer C.B. Flockhart, would be making the break to join him in February. The arrangement was that, if the committee heard nothing from Grimson before the 18 February they would assume the coast was clear for Flockhart to join him. They had no reply from him before the appointed day so Flockhart escaped. Only shortly after he had escaped the committee received a message from Grimson saying that it was clear for the man to come to him.

The following day Munkert got a letter from Grimson asking him to meet him in Memel the same day at 6.30 p.m. Munkert kept the appointment and they met. The escape committee was anxious for news of how Grimson was progressing in setting up an escape route and urged Munkert to get a full report. When they had found a suitably safe place to talk, Grimson told his story. Since leaving the Pole's house he had spent most of his time travelling on a grand tour of the Baltic ports, snatching only a few hours sleep in railway waiting-rooms or while he was on journeys. But while not on the move he had sought refuge at the home of the forester's brother. Here he had been well looked after and had actually succeeded in getting food coupons by trading for them with the supplies he had got from the camp. He went on to ask Munkert if he could arrange for some clothing to be passed on to him for the Pole who had helped him so much. (This was later done, much to the delight of the Pole.)

Grimson's most important discovery during his sojourns was the Swedish minister. He had succeeded in contacting him but to his surprise found the man far from willing to help. This discovery did little to hearten Grimson who was depending upon help from the man. However he had made contact with several others only too glad to help. They were, in the main, Polish workers and outlaws. Having given Munkert all the information he could, Grimson bade him farewell and they parted.

Munkert reported back to the escape committee while Grimson returned to the forester's house to await the arrival of Flockhart. On the 21st, Flockhart arrived at the house of the forester's brother. Grimson had been trying for some time to arrange a passage to Sweden for Flockhart but had drawn a blank. He thought, however, that there was a chance that something could be arranged from Danzig where he knew there were quite a number of Swedish ships which called there regularly.

That day, Grimson and Flockhart made their separate ways to Danzig and met up in the main railway station. Together they headed for the docks, an area which Grimson had reconnoitred several times and knew well. After a short search they found a Swedish ship being loaded with coal. It was guarded by a lone German sentry and there were quite a number of dock workmen busy on her. The two men arranged that Flockhart would wait where he was until an opportunity arose for him to board the ship. If a chance did not present itself then they would meet up again in the railway station waiting-room before dawn the following morning.

Flockhart lay in wait all night but the sentry was vigilant and did not leave his post once. The first light of day would soon be creeping over the docks so he decided it was time to leave. Grimson and he met up in the railway station and discussed their next move. Attempting to board the ship in daylight was courting disaster but Grimson thought of another approach. Since the landward side of the ship was heavily guarded he decided to have a crack at boarding her from the other side, using a rowing boat to get them there. They would, he said, have a try at his scheme the following night. In the meantime he would scout around the docks in search of a suitable rowing boat while Flockhart travelled to Gdynia to reconnoitre the docks and discover if there were any neutral ships in port.

Later that day the two men met up again when Flockhart returned from Gdynia. He had been unable to penetrate the dock area because it was strongly guarded and Grimson had also had a disappointing day. He had not found a rowing boat but had instead discovered another Swedish ship and one which seemed as if it might be considerably easier to board.

That night they returned to the Danzig docks and walked towards a hole in the dock perimeter fence which ran along the landward side of the docks and close to where the ship was berthed. Leaving Grimson to continue walking along the road, Flockhart slipped through the gap where he found two Swedish ships, the nearest one of which was guarded by a sentry. He scrambled in amongst some stationary railway goods wagons and examined the two ships. The nearer one was the larger of the two and he selected that as his target.

The sentry paced his beat along the ship's length then Flockhart saw his chance. As the German walked away from the gangway Flockhart, trying as best he could to look casual, slipped out from the railway wagons and sauntered towards it. But when he was only a few feet from the gangway, the sentry turned and spotted him. Flockhart dared not make a dash for it so he casually looked around him then strolled away in the opposite direction. The sentry was just about to shout to him when two Swedish sailors arrived to board the ship and while he was examining their papers, Flockhart made off and scrambled back out into the road.

Flockhart returned to the railway station waiting-room where he spotted Grimson waiting for him but rather than approach him they waited in separate parts of the room until morning when they left and Flockhart was able to tell him what had happened. They talked at length about the possibilities of boarding the ship in daylight and arrived at a scheme which they thought might work.

The idea was that Flockhart would board the ship dressed as a workman, but the only problem with this method was clothing. Somehow they had to lay their hands on a set of workman's clothes. Grimson, however, thought he might just be able to get what was required from one of his contacts. He left Flockhart and returned to the waiting-room two hours later with a complete set of overalls, a black cap of the type usually worn by workmen and a badge which all Polish workmen wore. Grimson passed the parcel of clothes over to Flockhart who disappeared into the toilet and did a quick change act then emerged clad in the garb of a Polish workman. His boiler suit hid the civilian clothes which he wore underneath. Grimson passed him his raincoat then with a final 'good luck' they parted.

Flockhart boarded a tram then a ferry to the dock area and returned to the hole in the fence which he slipped through and made his way to a workman's hut near the larger of the two Swedish ships. There he hid the suit-case he had been carrying. He noticed a gang of Russian prisoners helping with the loading of the ship under the watchful eye of a German guard and he loitered nearby hoping to enlist the aid of one of the Russians in boarding the ship but an opportunity did not present itself.

Flockhart noticed that the German sentry on the quay paced his beat regularly, walking exactly the same distance and over the same ground each time so he decided to try and pull off the same ruse he'd used before. He made his way back to the workman's hut and removed the Polish badge from his overalls then crept up to the ship hidden by the leg of a giant crane out of view of the sentry. The sentry's back was turned and he slipped out of hiding and began to examine one of the ship's mooring ropes. When the sentry finally turned and caught sight of Flockhart he must have assumed that he had every right to be there for he did nothing but continued on his beat. Relieved that the alarm had not been raised, Flockhart made his way to another of the mooring ropes, this time nearer the gangway up to the ship and he examined this one as well.

Out of the corner of his eye, he saw the sentry turn on his beat. Now was his chance to act and he walked on to the gangway and slowly up it on to the deck. He'd made it. Once on board Flockhart found a hiding place and the following day the ship sailed from Danzig. When a suitable time had elapsed, he emerged from his hiding place and gave himself up to the captain. Flockhart was treated with every hospitality by the captain and when the ship arrived in Stockholm, he was handed over to the police who took him to the British legation there. Less than a fortnight later he was back in England. Grimson's first charge had reached his goal.

While Flockhart had been making his way to England, Grimson was hard at work, paving the way for other escapers. He had found himself rented accommodation and had even gone to the extent of renting yet another two rooms which he stocked with food to be used by future escapers on the run. His biggest problem was getting food which he had to obtain through the black market and the price he had to pay was high. He paid frequent visits to Hydekrug to contact Munkert and get up-to-date information on the situation in the camp and the prospect of further escapes.

As the days and weeks passed, his organisation grew. He enlisted the help of Polish and foreign workers who lived and worked in Danzig. He devised a clever system of rendezvous with escapers. Grimson arranged to be at Danzig railway station every day between the hours of 12 noon and 1 p.m. and again between 7.30 p.m. and 8.30 p.m. All the escaper was required to do was to be there during either of these times and make contact with Grimson who would take him to hiding in one of his rented rooms. If the escaper could not be there during either of these times, he was to make his way to the docks where he would find a ferry time-table and place a mark against the time when he could be at the station. Grimson had enlisted the help of a Pole whose job it was to keep watch on the time-table and warn Grimson if a mark had been made.

By the end of March every detail had been taken care of and Grimson informed the escape committee by way of Munkert that he was ready to accept escapers, whenever they cared to make the break. He heard in reply that one man would make the break on 6 April but it was thought more advisable for Grimson to come to Hydekrug on that day and pick him up after he had broken out.

The escape committee felt that it was not enough to have just one escape route and two more prisoners volunteered to escape and set up another route, this time through Lithuania. They were Warrant Officer Townsend-Coles and Aircraftman Gewelber. Their plan was to establish a route through that country which would enable escapers either to reach the Russian lines or travel to neutral Sweden by fishing boat.

With the help of Munkert, the two men broke out of the camp and headed for Lithuania. They had been told beforehand that if they were unsuccessful in establishing a route, they were to wait for two weeks then travel to Danzig and contact Grimson. The Lithuanian frontier was only a few miles from the camp and after the escape they reached it but found it almost impassable because of the marshy country all around. Getting across it was hopeless and they agreed it was most prudent to head straight for Danzig and meet up with Grimson. But when they eventually arrived there, they could find no trace of him, in spite of the use of the time-table. While they were pondering on what had become of him, Grimson was in fact in Hydekrug waiting for the escaper he was to escort but the break-out had to be called off because of a last-minute hitch and was postponed till 13 April.

Grimson returned to Danzig but still there was no link-up between him and the two prisoners who had already escaped. He returned to Hydekrug on the 13th shortly after learning from one of his Polish helpers that Townsend-Coles and Gewelber had arrived. When he reached Hydekrug he met Munkert who told him that disaster had struck. The prisoner who had attempted to break out had been arrested and was being interrogated by the German Security Officer and the Criminal Police. Worse still, he had been carrying documents similar to those used by Grimson and that made Grimson's stay in Hydekrug decidedly unhealthy. The escape committee warned Grimson to get out as fast as he could, return to Danzig and lie low until the heat was off. After arranging to return to Hydekrug on 29 April, Grimson got out of the town with all haste.

When he arrived back in Danzig, he made contact

with the two escapers and learned that while they had been waiting in Danzig to make contact Gewelber had, in frustration, boldly approached a group of Polish sailors and admitted who he was. Luckily for him the Poles were sympathetic and they hid both men in their homes and subsequently in a work-camp for some days. In spite of the personal danger he was in, Grimson determined that he would get the two men out of the country and decided to try the previously successful method Flockhart had used. On 19 April he led them to the docks and the hole in the fence.

Grimson and the two others crept through the hole in the fence. They could see a sentry posted on duty by a Swedish ship in dock. Hastily Grimson made the arrangements. He would approach the sentry and engage him in conversation, diverting his attention from the gangway. When he turned his back, that would be the signal for the two escapers to slip on board.

The plan was simple and straightforward so Grimson left them and approached the sentry. While he was talking Townsend-Coles went first and, walking at a brisk pace, reached the gangway and began to scramble up it. Gewelber kept his distance and walked more slowly and it is as well that he did for the sentry spotted Townsend-Coles scrambling up the gangway and went after him, shouting at him to halt. By then Townsend-Coles was on the deck and bolting for cover. The sentry went in pursuit.

Gewelber was by then beside Grimson at the foot of the gangway.

'Now's your chance,' Grimson urged and with the sentry out of sight, Gewelber darted on board and disappeared.

Moments later the sentry re-appeared with Townsend-Coles. He'd been caught but Gewelber had got clean away. In spite of a German search of the ship, he was not discovered and reached Sweden from where he was repatriated the following month. Townsend-Coles, however, was not so fortunate. He was frog-marched off for questioning and later taken to a prison in Marienburg.

It was from this time on that things began to go seriously wrong. In the Hydekrug camp, the escape committee put a stop to all escapes for the time being. The prisoner who had attempted to escape on 6 April had undergone intensive questioning and the camp was searched thoroughly time and again. Worse still, although he had made an attempt to destroy his documents by throwing them in a fire, the would-be escaper had failed to do so and they were retrieved from the flames by the Germans. They were near perfect documents with excellent photographs on them and this led the authorities to suspect Sommers, the camp photographer, of complicity. He was questioned but claimed that he knew nothing of the photographs or how the prisoners had managed to take them. Although for the moment he was allowed to go free, he was still under suspicion and a close watch was kept on his movements.

Munkert, too, was being watched. The security staff had known that he was on friendly terms with the man who had tried to escape and suspected him of playing some part in the attempt. But for the time being at least he was not questioned. Throughout the camp there was a tense air of expectation. Everyone felt the balloon was about to go up. The prisoners could sense it and there was growing concern for Grimson who was unaware of developments at the camp.

The apprehension was well founded, for at that very time security men and Gestapo agents throughout the country were carrying out a search for Grimson and were closing in fast. He was then keeping a close watch on Townsend-Coles and careless of his own safety he actually waited in Marienburg, anxious to help Townsend-Coles if the chance arose.

Meanwhile in the camp things were hotting up at an alarming rate. The net was closing in on the collaborators. The escape committee tried desperately to warn Grimson to get out of the country by giving Munkert a note to that effect but it is not known whether or not Grimson actually received the warning.

On 21 April Sommers was escorted under heavy armed guard into the main compound at Hydekrug and all the occupants of one of the barrack blocks ordered to parade. Sommers was led along the rows of men while the guards waited for him to pick out those who had been implicated in the escape attempt. It was obvious to all of them that Sommers was under arrest. The Pole knew perfectly well the men who had been responsible but courageously, he picked none of them out and was led off back to gaol. There he was brought face to face with the man who had made the attempt but neither man claimed to recognise the other.

Sommers' fate seemed sealed when, a few days later, a member of the Polish Underground was shot dead by German police and on his body was found a note which mentioned Sommers by name—damning evidence against the man. It was clear that Sommers would be handed over to the Gestapo for interrogation. He had been in their hands once before and he knew perfectly well that this time they would use their vilest methods to get him to talk. He realised that he could not withstand that sort of torture and would inevitably talk. There seemed to be only one course open to him if he were to save his friends. By way of one of the guards who was also a collaborator, he got a message through to the escape committee telling them of his plight and asking them to smuggle him a phial of poison.

The escape committee was faced with a painful

decision. There was nothing they could do for the man. They could not hope to rescue him and they had to think of the many other people whom Sommers knew of and whose lives would be in danger if he talked. After a lengthy debate, they decided to comply with Sommers' request and the poison was smuggled in to him. The following day the escape committee learned that he had died during the night. A courageous man had sacrificed his life—but there were to be more lives lost in the same cause ...

The Polish guard who had arranged for Grimson to stay at his brother's house was also arrested. Luckily for the escape committee this man knew very little of their escape arrangements and could have told the Gestapo little. He, too, paid the supreme penalty and who knows what terrible ordeal he underwent before he was allowed the relief of death.

A few days later a note was handed to the escape committee by a German guard whom they suspected of being a 'plant', supposedly friendly to the prisoners and willing to help but in fact a loyal German bent on uncovering the organisation. The note was from Munkert and in it he claimed that, although he had been questioned by the security staff, he had managed to clear himself of suspicion. The escape committee were instantly on their guard. Had the note been delivered by anyone else they would have accepted it as bona fide but coming from this man whom they suspected of duplicity, they had to be wary.

In the note, Munkert asked for instructions on how to go about meeting Grimson on the 29th as arranged. Was this a German trick to catch Grimson red-handed and had Munkert talked? The committee had no way of confirming their suspicions but after lengthy discussions they decided to take a chance. At all costs Grimson had to be warned of the danger he was in so they wrote a note in reply, warning him to flee the country with all haste and they enclosed a large sum of money with the note. A further note was enclosed written by a close friend of Grimson and this one was signed by him while the other one remained unsigned. The committee took great pains in compiling the note to ensure that none of the Germans who had helped them was mentioned in it. The two notes and the money were handed back to Munkert's messenger on 29 April. He was not seen again.

That afternoon, Munkert was arrested and later that day news reached the escape committee that Grimson had been arrested at Insterburg. In a country-wide sweep the Gestapo rounded up all the Polish people who had given help to the committee and none of them was ever seen again. What happened to these courageous and unfortunate people is not known but it takes little imagination, knowing the ruthlessness with which the Gestapo acted, to summarise what became of them.

Townsend-Coles was brought back to Hydekrug and placed in solitary confinement in the camp gaol. Try as they might, the other prisoners could not get near him. He was, it seemed, in a particularly perilous situation since he had been caught wearing civilian clothes and therefore was quite likely to be shot as a spy. He was saved from immediate execution only by the fact that he had had the sense to keep with him his prisoner-of-war identity disc.

One day the guards swept into the camp and arrested six of the prisoners, including the member of the escape committee who had written the note to Grimson. They were put into solitary in the camp gaol and it was then that Grimson's friend managed to snatch a few words with Townsend-Coles. He learned that the courageous Grimson had actually travelled on the same train as he when he was escorted back to Hydekrug from Marienburg, but neither man had been able to make contact with the other because of the heavy guard escorting Townsend-Coles. The last he had seen of Grimson was at Insterburg when he was arrested.

Townsend-Coles was removed from Stalag Luft 6 on 6 May and taken to Tilsit Civil Prison where he was charged with espionage and working in collaboration with the Polish Underground Movement. On 15 July, 1944, so the Germans claimed, he had 'offered resistance' while at Tilsit and been shot dead by a guard. In his book *Escape From Germany* *, Aidan Crawley states that '... the British Government demanded an inquiry but before this could be carried out by the Protecting Power the area was occupied by Russian forces and no further investigation was possible.'

What became of Warrant Officer Grimson, the man who had so courageously and unselfishly remained in enemy territory relinquishing his own freedom that others could escape, is uncertain. He was never seen again by any of his prison comrades and an informant told them that he had been executed by the Germans shortly after his arrest. Knowing as we do now the change in the Germans' attitude towards escaping prisoners and their collaborators at that stage of the war, there can be little doubt that what the informant claimed was true.

* Published in 1956 by Collins.

# 3

# *Exit a Prisoner*

Throughout the Second World War, many thousands of German soldiers, sailors and airmen were held captive in prisoner-of-war camps in the more remote regions of the British Isles, notably Wales, Scotland and the Lake District. Although many of them succeeded in breaking out of their camps, not one of them actually left Britain's shores and returned to Germany.

In the early days of the war, few of them even attempted to escape but this reluctance to make the break is perhaps understandable when one considers that they had been promised by no less a personage than Hitler himself that Britain would be crushed within weeks. All they were required to do, they reasoned, was to wait for the successful completion of 'Operation Sealion', the invasion of Britain. The armed might of the Third Reich would be unleashed upon the United Kingdom and the island nation crushed into defeat. Why risk life and limb in a bid for freedom when rescue was only weeks away? As the war progressed, however, the seeds of doubt were sewn in their minds when the promised invasion did not come. By then the British were shipping their prisoners off across the North Atlantic to camps deep in the heart of Canada.

Unlike British and Allied prisoners of war held captive in Germany, the German prisoner of war had no neutral countries near at hand into which he could make his dash. Nor was there any chance of help from a sympathetic Underground Movement for there was no such thing in Britain. There were Nazi sympathisers, but they were securely behind bars out of harm's way. The German prisoner of war, if he succeeded in escaping in Britain, was faced with a population utterly hostile to him; one which would do all in its power to put him back where he had come from—behind the wire.

In spite of all the difficulties which lay in the path of the German escaper, there was one young officer who probably came closer to succeeding than any other. He was Oberleutnant Baron Franz von Werra, a dashing, handsome young Luftwaffe fighter pilot who had already made a name for himself in the Fatherland as a leading fighter ace—a claim to fame he was later to regret bitterly.

Von Werra had all the story-book qualities of the typical German fighter pilot. He was titled, with a good pedigree—or at least so he claimed.* He exuded an air of daring and was a 'line-shooter' almost without peer. Although he did not sport the requisite duelling scar on his cheek, which would have completed the Germanic image, he had the required physical deformity in that the index finger of his right hand remained permanently straight. Above all he was the personification of charm, a man whose personality made him liked instantly by all he met—including his eventual captors. To round off the image, and to out-do his fellow pilots, he kept a tame lion cub as a pet.

By the time the Battle of Britain had reached its peak in September 1940, von Werra claimed to have shot down five British aircraft and destroyed eight others on the

* In the book *The One That Got Away*, written by Kendal Burt and James Leasor, published in 1956 by Collins & Michael Joseph, the joint authors prove that in fact von Werra was not entitled to the title 'baron'.

ground, a total which placed him among the leading aces in the Luftwaffe. His claim, however, was almost completely false since in one encounter with the R.A.F. over England, he was said to have boldly 'tagged-on' to the end of a flight of British fighters landing at their base and shot down three of them while they were touching down, then strafed some more on the ground. (It was later proved beyond doubt that no such incident had ever taken place—a fact which was to cause von Werra considerable embarrassment when he eventually fell into British hands.)

Von Werra was a national hero but his fame was based on falsehoods concocted by the 'ace' himself. He revelled in the publicity showered on him in the German press and enjoyed the adoration of his fellow pilots. He kept up his story of his daring exploits over Britain. After all who could prove him false?—only the British, and his countrymen were hardly likely to take their word for it. But the vain young Luftwaffe pilot's ego was soon to take a nasty knock when on 5 September, 1940, at a time when the Battle of Britain was at its fiercest, his Messerschmitt Bf 109 fighter was forced down over southern England.

The 5th September was a sweltering hot day in England with a clear blue sky scarred by the white vapour trails streaming after the fighters and bombers doing battle high above the green countryside. Von Werra's Messerschmitt was among those that duelled with the R.A.F. Spitfires and Hurricanes wheeling about the sky with machine-guns chattering until suddenly his engine gave a cough and began to splutter. The 109 lost height quickly tumbling towards the ground, chased by a Spitfire hell-bent on a kill but the German succeeded in evading the streams of bullets that laced through the air and zipped past his machine.

Von Werra's eyes scanned the fields below, picking one

out for a forced landing. Escape was impossible in his crippled machine and he levelled out only a hundred feet above the ground and jived about the sky, fighting to maintain height until he reached the green field ahead of him. The fighter skipped across the tree tops watched by the crew of a searchlight battery on the ground. A gunner grabbed the Lewis gun sighted there and fired long bursts of bullets at the machine as it swept past.

The field was just ahead as von Werra cut the power from his engine and the plane slithered on to the ground. The rotating propeller bit into the grass gouging great chunks out of the field and spraying them into the air as von Werra braced himself against the impact. At last the fighter slid to a halt and von Werra threw open the canopy and jumped out. Even as he hit the ground, a group of soldiers armed with rifles were darting across the field towards him. His first thought was to make a dash for it but escape was hopeless. Instead he took some papers from his pocket and set fire to them, making sure that they would not fall into the hands of the enemy. Soon he was surrounded by soldiers waving their rifles menacingly in his face. With that he was led off to captivity.

Von Werra was unceremoniously bundled into the back of an army lorry then taken off to the police station at Maidstone, Kent, where he was locked up but not before, true to form, signing the autograph book of the police sergeant's son. It seemed that, even as a prisoner, the German had an eye for publicity!

The following day von Werra was released from his cell and under armed guard taken by truck to London. In due course, the truck arrived at a heavily guarded mansion in Kensington Palace Gardens. Although von Werra did not know it, this was the London District Prisoner-of-War Cage where he was to get his first real taste of what it was like to be a prisoner of war.

Von Werra could never have foreseen what was in

store for him. The Luftwaffe had taken few precautions in teaching their pilots how to behave under interrogation. They had been told to give only their names, ranks and serial numbers—and nothing else. They had not been warned of the subtlety of the British interrogators' techniques. Without getting answers to direct questions, an interrogator could get a vast amount of information merely by talking about seemingly innocent subjects and drawing a prisoner into a conversation, catching him off guard. The interrogators were highly skilled judges of character and changed their techniques to suit the man they were questioning.

Von Werra underwent two major sessions of interrogation at the London Cage and was shaken rigid when he discovered just how much information the British had on him. Not only did they know that he was of Swiss origin and had no real claim to the title 'Baron', they were able to tell him his squadron number, the names of the pilots in his squadron, the name of the base from which he operated, his commanding officer's name, the fact that he had a pet lion called Simba and also show him pictures of himself and articles about him cut from *current* German newspapers.

The German had at all times until then remained aloof but his arrogance was dealt a shattering blow when an R.A.F. interrogator demolished his story about how he claimed to have shot down the three Hurricanes over the British airfield then destroyed many more on the ground. Von Werra's confidence was crushed in one swift, sure stroke. The R.A.F. officer was quick to point out that if he were to let it be known amongst the German officers with whom he would be imprisoned that his claim was a pack of lies and that the so-called 'ace' was no more than a compulsive line-shooter, life in the prisoner-of-war camp would be hell for him. The interrogator used this as a lever to get information out of Von Werra but it is to the

German's credit that in spite of the threat, he refused point blank to help the British in any way.

Von Werra's interrogation continued for many days but to his surprise the British at no time resorted to violence of any kind to get their information. They used almost every other device in the book, from the most subtle techniques already described to planting microphones, some of which were dummies to throw the prisoner off the scent of the real ones. They even resorted to the old trick of putting a phoney Luftwaffe pilot in von Werra's cell in a bid to lure him into conversation on secret matters. Von Werra, however, soon led him up the garden path, knowing full well that he was not who he said he was. Somehow his story just did not ring true. Von Werra later discovered that this particular 'German' officer was a man of many talents, changing his name, identity and service to suit the particular prisoner who was in captivity. He had been a U-boat commander, a fighter pilot and an officer of the Wehrmacht!

During his stay at the London Cage and subsequently at another cage in Cockfosters, von Werra continually pestered all and sundry, anxious to know when he would be transferred to a permanent prisoner-of-war camp. This thought was uppermost in his mind for it was clear to him that it would only be then that he could get down to the business of escape. Unlike many of his fellow officers he did not share the belief that rescue was near at hand when the promised invasion came. He was determined to get back to Germany as soon as possible.

It was not until the end of September that von Werra was at last taken under guard to a train bound for the Lake District. After what seemed like an eternity, he arrived at Grizedale Hall, a gaunt stone-built mansion set in a Lancashire valley just south of Hawkshead and a mile north of the little village of Satterthwaite. Known amongst the locals as 'U-boat Hotel', it boasted forty rooms and was by comparison to German prisoner-of-war camps a palace. It was typical of the old English stately home, dark and demure with imposing stained glass windows which cut out most of the light. Outside, the Hall was heavily guarded and surrounded by a dense barbed wire entanglement with a number of nissen huts built to house the army staff.

Von Werra was shepherded in and shown his quarters, a small but comfortable room with only the barest furnishings. After the initial formalities of introduction to his new 'home' had been completed, von Werra met the other prisoners, amongst them many old friends whom he had thought were dead. He was greeted warmly by his old comrades and introduced to the senior German officer Major Willibald Fanelsa.

The newcomer wasted no time in informing Fanelsa of his intention to escape at the earliest opportunity but his suggestion was met by peals of laughter from the other inmates, most of whom had already investigated the possibility and given it up as hopeless. The odds were weighted heavily against success. Even if he did succeed in getting out of the Hall, where would he go? The area was surrounded by mile upon mile of desolate moorland which afforded no cover for the escaper and he could expect no help from the population. Then he would be faced with the problem of how to get out of England. The only remote possibility would be by stowing away on a neutral ship but the docks were very heavily guarded.

In spite of the pessimistic attitude adopted by his fellow officers, von Werra was not to be deterred. He was resolute in his purpose and determined that he would succeed where others before him had failed. For the next ten days, von Werra spent all his time spying out the lie of the land, noting every detail that could be of use to him. As he did so a plan was forming in his mind.

There was one 'chink' in the British armour which he

thought might give him the chance he needed to effect an escape. In order to give the prisoners the required amount of exercise as laid down in the international rules governing the treatment of prisoners of war, they were taken on walks three or four times a week *outside the camp*. The party generally consisted of two dozen prisoners marching in three ranks with four guards in the lead, four taking up the rear, a sergeant on horseback and an officer in charge. There were only two routes taken by the party, either up the road which passed the main gate or down it to the south and through the village of Satterthwaite.

The procedure followed on these marches was always the same. The prisoners were marched for about a mile then they stopped for a rest before returning to camp. The route to the north held little hope since it took them into barren moorland but the south route had possibilities for escape since there were fields and woods which afforded some cover. Von Werra's plan depended on them being taken on the south route.

Von Werra knew that his escape would be no walk-over. Security during the march was tight; the guards were keen-eyed and the sergeant on horseback rode continually up and down the ranks of men, checking them as he did so. There was, however, one point when the guards were not perhaps quite as vigilant as usual and that was during the rest period. On the south route they always stopped at the same place, a bend in the road, with trees on one side and a low wall on the other which skirted a field. Generally the prisoners sat against the wall or on top of it while the guards and mounted sergeant took up positions on the other side of the road from where they could watch the prisoners. Perhaps the most important feature of the rest was the fact that the sergeant generally dismounted. This meant that he no longer had such a good view of the prisoners and that, von Werra decided, would be the time to strike. If only he could get over the wall, he could be out of sight of the guards and wait there until they had gone.

There was one further difficulty. Immediately after the rest period, the prisoners were counted before starting off. Everything would depend upon the other Germans in the party fooling the guards into thinking they still had twenty-four men. The whole plan required the co-operation of his friends and strict timing if it were to be a success.

Von Werra put his plan to the senior officers who considered it then gave it their blessing. They agreed that the sheer audacity of it might just pull it off and they offered von Werra all the help they could muster. For a disguise von Werra would wear his short, leather jacket without its badges of rank and a pair of leather trousers given him by a U-boat officer. Food it seemed would be the greatest problem. He couldn't carry a bag for this would be spotted by the guards. Anything he took with him he would have to carry on his person as inconspicuously as possible. He had saved all his chocolate ration which would keep him going for a few days and he had acquired some English money which he hoped to use to buy food. He had left little to chance and had a small home-made compass together with a rough map of the area.

Another great problem would be the concentration of British troops in the area, all waiting in readiness for the threatened invasion. Many hundreds of them could be called upon to carry out a search for him but even this did not deter him.

On Monday, 7 October, only twelve days after his arrival at Grizedale Hall, all was ready for von Werra's escape attempt. He had asked the senior German officer to persuade the commandant to have the march in the afternoon, making the excuse that it was interfering with educational classes. The commandant agreed, unaware, of course, that the real reason was that by escaping in the afternoon, von Werra would have only a short time to wait until nightfall.

At 2 p.m. the party of prisoners set off with the usual number of guards. As they marched out of the gate, the column swung south. This was exactly what von Werra wanted. So far, so good and off they marched, down through the village until at last they reached the rest point. It was now or never, he thought. Two of the prisoners draped their coats over the wall as arranged and von Werra casually hoisted himself on to the wall and lay along it with his hands clasped beneath his head as if having a snooze. The mounted sergeant and the guards took up their usual positions at the other side of the road. Nothing seemed out of the ordinary, except that von Werra's heart was pounding like an engine.

Von Werra lay there waiting for the signal from two of his accomplices who were keeping a close watch on the scene in front of them, waiting for the moment when von Werra could disappear. But moments later, a horse and cart came trundling along the road. Von Werra saw it and realised that the man at the reins would have a perfect view of him if he dropped off the wall. His plan, he thought, was ruined. But far from hindering him, the cart actually proved to be a help because when it pulled level with them it obscured the prisoners from the guards. This was it. One of the lookouts gave him a nudge and he slid off the wall and crouched behind it. His timing was perfect and no one noticed his disappearance when the cart drew away.

Minutes later, the sergeant ordered the prisoners to form up in ranks but as they shuffled into some semblance of order von Werra was spotted, not by the guards but by two women working in the field into which he had dropped. They waved madly to the guards as von Werra darted along the side of the wall, cursing them as he went. It seemed that the game was up—but far from it. The Germans realised what had happened and they waved back to the women as if returning a friendly greeting. The guards barked at the prisoners to get back into line and the column began to move off. Try as they might, the women could not make the guards realise what had happened.

As arranged, when the column moved off, the Germans purposely straggled their ranks making it impossible for the sergeant to carry out a proper count of them and at the same time they burst into song—a signal to von Werra that he had not been discovered. The sergeant was quickly losing his temper as the men jinked about in the road. Then in frustration, he called them to a halt. It was then he discovered that one of them was missing. Rifles were raised and the muzzles waved in the faces of the prisoners. It was a tense moment; tempers were frayed and anything could happen. The number was checked and sure enough one had got away. With that the sergeant galloped off up the road to raise the alarm at the camp but by then von Werra was well under way.

Von Werra ran for some distance along by the wall then peered over it to see that the coast was clear. Satisfied that it was safe, he scrambled across and dived into the woods on the other side. Wasting no time he got to his feet and with all his might struggled through the undergrowth and through the trees, panting with exhaustion as he fought his way up the steep incline. He paused only once to glance back and see whether or not he was being followed. But all was silent in the woods. On he charged up the hill until he at last reached the summit where he stopped again. He'd made it, he thought. But he paused only long enough to catch his breath then he dashed on, racing as fast as he could along the edge of woods until at last, just after five o'clock, he could go on no longer and he scurried into a wood and lay down to sleep.

By this time the countryside was alive with troops, searching hill and dale, tramping over the wild moorland and beating the brush. The placid countryside was transformed into a seething mass of khaki uniforms. Lorries loaded with troops, careered down country lanes at breakneck speed, racing to points where the escaper was thought to be. The police forces of three counties were alerted. Photographs and descriptions of von Werra were flashed across the country. The B.B.C. warned the entire country of the prisoner's escape. All Britain was on the lookout for him but search as they might they could find no trace of the fugitive. Von Werra had disappeared as if into thin air.

It rained almost continually for days on end while troops and policemen scoured the countryside in search of the escaper. On the wild moorland and in the dense woods, troops searched day and night for von Werra. Nothing was left to chance and every nook and cranny was explored thoroughly but the elusive von Werra was still at large. How could a man survive in such appalling conditions? He would have to find some shelter and yet every farm, outhouse or shepherd's shelter had been searched at least once. His strength must be waning since there was little food around which he could get to keep him alive. He could, of course, have been dead by then, lying in some bog which had been missed. But as it turned out, von Werra was far from dead ...

On the evening of 10th October, three days after his escape, von Werra sought rest in a stone-built shelter high on a fell not far from the coast. He was soaked through and covered from head to toe in thick mud. Exhausted but satisfied that he had so far managed to elude his searchers, he settled down; then only an hour from midnight he heard a noise outside. Someone was approaching and he peered round the open door. He saw two dark shapes moving through the rain towards the hut. He was cornered. For three days he had watched his searchers miss him sometimes only by yards but now he was truly caught. In the half light that filtered through the door he caught sight of a large chunk of wood lying on the floor and he grabbed it, determined to put up a fight if he were discovered. As the two men drew nearer he retreated into the shadows within the hut and waited, his heart thumping with expectation.

The two men, both members of the Home Guard, were armed, one with a shotgun and the other with a revolver. They, like many hundreds of other searchers, had been out every night scouring the countryside and had almost given up hope of finding their man. This shelter was like many others they had explored in the course of their hunt and there was nothing to outwardly suggest that anyone was inside, but nevertheless they approached it with caution, drawing their weapons as they shone their lamp into the door.

They stopped in their tracks as the light from their torch fell on the dishevelled figure crouched in the corner of the shelter. It was their man all right and they levelled their guns at him. They could see from the state of the man that he had no fight left in him but they were taking no chances. One of them tied a cord round von Werra's right wrist and took a firm grip of the other end then motioned to him to get out.

The rain was still teeming down and the hillside was slippery as they made their way down it. They had not gone far when von Werra gave an almighty tug on the cord, loosening it from his wrist. The sudden jerk unbalanced his captor who tumbled to the ground dropping the lamp he was carrying which hit the ground and went out. Plunged into darkness, the time was ripe to make a dash for it and in the bewildering moments of surprise that had caught his captors off guard, he scrambled off up the hill and disappeared into the darkness. The two guards regaining their composure, gave chase but they had lost him and realising this they hurriedly made off down the hill to raise the alarm.

Von Werra it seemed had got clean away, for the searchers hunted for two more days without a sign of him. More troops were poured into the area but it seemed that the cunning escaper had managed to slip through the net. Then on the afternoon of Sunday, the 13th, the lucky break came ...

A whole gang of searchers had been hard at it all day searching in the area of the Eskdale road but they had met with no success until, while they were resting, one of them spotted a man, high up on a nearby hill shouting and waving his arms, trying to attract their attention. The soldiers and policemen leapt to their feet and charged up to where the man was standing. They recognised him as Mr William Youdale, a local farmer. He was out of breath but he quickly explained that only minutes before, he had seen a man not far from where he was standing who fitted the description of the escaper. Immediately the searchers spread out in a wide line and moved off to hunt him down. He could not have gone far but as the searchers swept the countryside there was no sign of him. It appeared that the farmer had been mistaken when the search went on and revealed nothing.

The ground in that part of the country afforded no cover at all since it was coated with short heather in which no one could successfully hide. They had gone quite a distance over the vast expanse of moorland when one of the searchers noticed a slight movement in a shallow bog only yards from where he walked. He and the others made their way to it and there, lying half submerged in muddy water, was von Werra. They had found him at last. He was hauled from the squelching mud and helped down the hill to a nearby pub where he was given a steaming hot cup of tea. Not long after, he was back at Grizedale Hall where the commanding officer sentenced him to twenty-one days solitary confinement for attempting to escape.

Throughout his term of solitary, von Werra was able to reflect upon his escape and his failure to pull it off successfully. He had gained a lot of very valuable information during his six days of freedom and he pondered on how it could be useful to him in the future. He was bitterly disappointed that he had failed but he was determined that he would try again and he applied his mind to how he could break out again. Nothing was going to deter von Werra but his plans were in for a knock. When he was released from solitary, he found that many of the prisoners had been transferred to another camp and he was ordered to get his things together. He was to follow them.

Under close guard, he was taken to a train which was to transport him to his new 'home'. He was worried about this change for he firmly believed that he was being sent to a punishment camp, with even tighter security specially reserved for troublesome prisoners.

Von Werra was right about the tighter security, as he found out when he arrived at Swanwick prisoner-of-war camp, situated about half-way between Derby and Chesterfield. Like Grizedale Hall, the new camp was a converted country house but on a much grander scale. It was known as The Hayes and was vast by comparison with von Werra's previous abode. It had more than two hundred rooms and various other buildings which housed the prison staff. The whole complex of buildings was surrounded by double barbed-wire fencing and high powerful lamps all around. There were to be no 'country walks' from this camp. There was a self-contained exercise ground in which the prisoners were given their daily dose of exercise. Dense woods skirted the main road leading to the double main gates and at the rear of the buildings was a wide meadow.

Escape from The Hayes was, it seemed, to be very much more difficult than from Grizedale Hall but von Werra refused to be put off and within the first few days he was reconnoitring the camp and sizing it up for a break-out. When he first arrived at the Swanwick cage, he had found many of the prisoners who had been with him at Grizedale Hall, including Major Fanelsa, who was again the senior German officer. Fanelsa seemed a changed man and he pointed out in no uncertain terms that von Werra should give up the idea of escaping—at least for the moment. He told von Werra that they had given the camp a thorough going over and found that escape was impossible. He had built up a reasonable relationship with the commandant which had resulted in them getting certain privileges and he did not want to lose these as a result of some hare-brained attempt at escape by von Werra. The intrepid escaper, however, was determined to try—with or without Fanelsa's consent.

Von Werra teamed up with some other prisoners who had the same thought in mind. They were Leutnant Wagner, Major Heinz Cramer, Leutnant Walter Manhard, Leutnant Wilhelm and Leutnant Malischewski. They held secret meetings during which they discussed the possibilities of escape and they soon reached the conclusion that there was only one way out—by tunnel, and they searched high and low for a suitable place to begin digging. They selected an unused room in the north wing of the building and their intention was that the end of the tunnel would be just outside the perimeter fence. Like all other tunnellers they were faced with the problem of how they were to dispose of the earth they took out of the ground. It was quite by chance that they found a solution ...

In captivity, men had to fight against their biggest

enemy—boredom—and they found many and varied ways of doing this. Some launched themselves into studies while others indulged in amateur dramatics. To while away the days many of them became physical fitness fanatics and Leutnant Manhard was one such devotee. He had been a heavyweight boxer before the war and he kept himself in trim by weight-lifting, picking up every heavy weight he could find to improve his strength. One day he was searching for a weight on which to test his strength when he spotted a likely one in the shape of a huge stone slab in front of a building known as the garden house, situated alongside the high wire fence. The slab was a challenge to him and he flexed his muscles and heaved on it. At first it would not be lifted then he gave it an almighty tug and it came away from the ground. There below it was a pit about six feet deep with water at the bottom of it. He quickly realised that he had found just what they had been looking for and he rushed to tell the others. They carried out an examination of this pit and discovered that it was in fact a vast water tank ideal as a place to deposit the earth they were to dig out of the tunnel. With that problem solved they turned their attentions to the tunnel proper and von Werra and Malischewski were elected to do the digging.

The tunnel would, of necessity, be a crude affair, gouged out of the earth and shored up only where absolutely necessary and only big enough for a man to scramble along it. The earth excavated from the tunnel would be carried to the underground reservoir by two men allotted to the task and a series of lookouts posted at strategic points would keep a weather eye open for guards. If the British got the slightest wind of the tunnel, their efforts would all have been in vain and it was vital that one man kept a constant watch on the surface of the ground under which the tunnel was being dug to make sure that there were no outward signs of what was going on below.

With everyone allotted to his individual task, the team of diggers and lookouts started work on 17th November. A key for the empty room from which the tunnel was to begin was 'acquired' and von Werra and his accomplice set to work on the parquet flooring. They moved the large locker from the corner of the room and levered up sections of the flooring, taking great care not to break any because they had to be replaced after each day's work was done. They gouged away at the breeze and the clinker underneath before coming to the soil, then the buckets of earth were 'spirited away' by carriers to disappear down the pit. Meanwhile a wooden frame was made which fitted neatly over the hole and could be removed or replaced with ease. With the preliminaries complete they got down to hacking away at the soil with crude instruments until after days of toil, they reached the one element they had prayed was not there beneath the earth—water. Von Werra had hoped to dig down at least ten feet before striking out underneath the fence but with water seeping in fast they had to make do with the tunnel being dug only six feet below the surface, which heightened the chances of discovery from the surface.

The tension suffered by all the men was telling, particularly on Malischewski who became so nervous about being discovered that he finally opted out of the scheme altogether. There was no room for the nervy type on this mission and his place was taken by the robust Manhard who launched himself into the work with gusto, doing much more than his fair share. The tunnel progressed but it was not without its moments of high tension and near disaster.

One day when the tunnel was fairly far advanced, the lookout in the empty room was shocked into fear when he heard a loud noise coming from the tunnel. He glanced over to a nearby guard and noticed that he too had heard it. Like a man possessed he switched on and off the primitive lighting system which had been installed in the tunnel and von Werra got the pre-arranged warning and scrambled back down the tunnel to emerge grimy-faced at the opening in the floor. Luckily the guards took no further notice but it had been a close shave. Had one of them come charging into the room to find out what was going on he'd have found von Werra resplendent in his working clothes—every inch a tunneller. It transpired that von Werra had come up against some solid sandstone and hacked away at it with a crow-bar using so much force that the noise was heard above ground. As a result of the narrow escape it was arranged that cover-noises would be laid on when the diggers came to a tricky part of the tunnel.

As the tunnel bit farther towards the fence they were faced with another hazard—suffocation. The lack of air made work almost impossible and the rate of progress slowed dramatically. Often they had to be dragged from the tunnel only half conscious and fighting for breath but they courageously battled on until they reached what appeared to be an insurmountable hazard—a drain pipe stretching right across their path.

Going underneath the pipe was out of the question because of the ever present threat of water and tunnelling over it was equally difficult because it brought the digging dangerously close to the surface and detection would be that much easier for the guards. It seemed that they had come to the bitter end. But after due discussion it was decided that they would have to go over the top. This necessitated some tricky digging for it meant sloping the tunnel in order to get over the obstacle and shoring it up very carefully. Gingerly they set about their task and were making good progress when one day as Manhard was digging there was an ominous rumble from the tunnel.

The horrible truth dawned immediately on von Werra. The tunnel had collapsed. He scrambled into it to reach his friend but it was pitch dark ahead. The fall of soil had covered the lamp. At last he reached Manhard's feet and he pulled with all his might but could not budge him. Frantically he clawed away at the earth with his bare hands until he had removed enough of it to pull the trapped man free. Manhard had been close to death but von Werra had got to him just in time. They struggled back down the tunnel until they reached the opening where both of them collapsed in a heap, fighting for breath.

At last when they had regained their breath they made their way down the tunnel once more and found to their delight that, far from proving a disaster, the fall of soil was their salvation. They found they could breathe fresh air. Ahead of them was part of a sunken barbed wire entanglement buried in clinker and the barbed wire had bound the clinker together and held it in position, preventing it from falling in on them completely. But furthermore, air was able to filter through the clinker and this would make the going very much easier.

The most startling discovery of all was the barbed wire itself. Their calculations had put them far short of the fence but the barbed wire indicated that they had in fact reached the perimeter fence and with renewed heart they got down to work again the following day. With the tunnel fast reaching the break-out point, they could now at last turn their attentions to the problem of how they were going to make their escape from England.

Von Werra had already given this a great deal of thought and planned to steal an aeroplane from an R.A.F. airfield and fly back to Germany taking with him an R.A.F. plane in the process! At first his suggestion was met by a howl of guffaws by his fellow conspirators but as he went on to explain his plan in detail they soon realised that he did have a fighting chance, at least as good as theirs. He planned to pose as a Dutchman, Captain van Lott, who had joined the R.A.F. and was flying bombers in a special mixed squadron of Coastal Command operating out of Dyce, near Aberdeen. Von Werra had thought it out carefully and chosen his false identity with care. He reasoned that the people on the airfield from which he chose to steal the plane would not be connected with Coastal Command since their field would be far inland. This being the case they would be far less likely to detect his false identity. He chose to be a Dutchman because, although he spoke excellent English, he did have a heavy accent and being a Dutchman would account for that. The operations of the special mixed squadrons were furthermore a mystery to many R.A.F. personnel since they were used on special operations only and von Werra could weave a credible tale by using his vivid imagination. He chose Dyce as his base partly because it was hundreds of miles from where he was likely to find his aerodrome and secondly because he had a fellow prisoner who knew the area around Dyce well and could furnish him with a fairly accurate description of it.

Von Werra had even concocted a story to tell the man who would question him when he reached his aerodrome. He would claim that he had been badly shot up in his Wellington bomber while on a raid on a Danish port and only just managed to limp back to Britain where he crash-landed near Derby. He would then have to 'play it by ear' weighing up the situation when he arrived at the R.A.F. base. He could not foretell how his story would be received by the staff at the R.A.F. aerodrome.

There was one major difficulty which had to be overcome and that was the manufacture of an identity disc. Von Werra would need one for it was certain that he would be asked to prove his identity. He would not require identity papers since he would claim that he was not allowed to carry them on secret missions but he did need a disc. He and his friends pondered on how they could lay their hands on one. None of them had any idea of what they looked like so they devised a cunning scheme to get a look at one.

Von Werra and his fellow conspirators collared one of the British cooks in the cook house one day and asked him to settle a bet they had. They claimed to have seen an identity disc on a captured airman and one of them said it had the owner's name, rank, number and religion on it, whilc the others believed that it did not have the owner's religion. The unsuspecting cook produced his own disc which the group scrutinised carefully before returning it. They had got the information they required. The disc had the cook's name, rank and religion but that was all.

Now that they had seen and felt the disc for size and weight, they had to set about making one. This was not to prove easy. It was made of a brownish vulcanised fibre which would be difficult to imitate. They tried linoleum but it proved unsuitable then they used thick cardboard but it was too light, so they overcame this by slicing a cardboard disc and inserting a piece of lead from a tooth-paste tube in between the two slices and pasting them together. The disc was suitably dyed to match the right colour then the required letters cut into it with the point of a nail file. It seemed that their ingenuity had paid off for it was a remarkable likeness and more were made for the others.

Of the other escapers, Cramer and Manhard were to stick together and try to hitch-hike to Scotland where they hoped to board a neutral ship while Wilhelm and Wagner were to make for Liverpool where they would try to board a ship bound for Eire.

The tunnel was progressing well and at last it reached a point behind a hedge outside the wire and out of view of the nearby watchtower. The time had come for the breakthrough and a night was selected for the escape. The work had taken one month and the escape was planned for the night of 17th December but there was an obstacle in their path—Major Fanelsa. Before breaking out they had to get his permission to go and at first he would not give it. His reason was that a Special Medical Commission was due to arrive at the camp to assess wounded prisoners for repatriation to Germany and he did not want to jeopardise their chances by having an escape on his hands, so he postponed the escape bid for three days. At last, however, the night came for the break.

Tension amongst the escapers was at its peak all day as the hour slowly crept near. Dusk came and soon the camp was in darkness, then fate played a kind hand in the operation when Luftwaffe bombers struck at Liverpool and Derby. To conform to the black-out rules the floodlighting which illuminated the camp was switched off. Now was the time to go.

The escapers made their way to the empty room which housed the tunnel entrance, each one clutching the few possessions he was to take with him. Von Werra was clad in a flying suit he had 'borrowed' and wore an old pair of pyjamas over it to protect it from the dirt in the tunnel. On his head he wore a small beret to avoid getting his hair dirty.

The motley crew of men clad in their varied assortment of clothing congregated in the room where Fanelsa wished them good luck. The tunnel cover was removed and von Werra, the first to go, dropped into it and slid into the tunnel, crawling along its length until he came to the end where he began hacking away at the surface. The work was agonising but at last the turf on the top came away and there above him he could see a circle of stars.

Gingerly he peered over the rim of the hole. All was quiet except for the air-raid which raged far off on the horizon. Summoning his strength, he hoisted himself out of the hole and into the darkness. Half crouched he slipped through the night towards a group of farm buildings nearby. Then he skirted them before stopping dead in his tracks when he heard a gate open and close. He was by the edge of a lane and could see a group of people starting to walk down the lane—*right towards him.*

At that, he was joined by Cramer and Manhard. Their hearts pounded as the four people came nearer to them. They couldn't fail to spot them. Discovery it seemed was inevitable. But moments later the four people halted, conferred with each other briefly then turned and retraced their steps back along the track in the direction from which they had come. The escapers could not believe their luck. They waited for a moment then darted across the lane to a barn which they had previously agreed would be their rendezvous. After a hasty round of handshaking, Cramer and Manhard departed into the night. Von Werra was alone. Then not long after, just as he too was about to leave, the other two arrived. There was no time for lengthy farewells and they departed swiftly. Von Werra then decided it was better to wait there in hiding until the all clear was given then he would set off. He crouched down, only two hundred yards from the prison camp from which he had escaped and waited. The all clear did not come until the early hours of the morning when von Werra left his hide and started off across the fields.

Little did von Werra know at the time but the search for him was already under way. Cramer was captured shortly after his escape and a check was carried out at the camp which revealed that five prisoners were missing. The hunt was on. (Wilhelm, Manhard and Wagner were later captured, leaving von Werra the only one still at large.)

Von Werra made his way cautiously along country lanes and across fields without encountering a single person until at last he reached a railway line. For a moment he stopped and listened and was sure he could hear the sound of a stationary locomotive not far off down the track. Somehow he had to make his first contact with the British so summoning his courage he made off along the track in the direction of the locomotive. Sure enough it was there and he clambered on to the footplate where he came face to face with a surprised driver.

The driver asked who he was and von Werra repeated his carefully rehearsed story, explaining that he was the pilot of a Wellington bomber which had crash-landed some distance away and he stressed the urgency of his need to reach an R.A.F. station as quickly as possible. He pointed out that he had to get to a telephone and enquired where he could find one. The driver told him that the nearest phone was at a station down the line and obligingly offered him the services of his fireman who was due to go off duty. The fireman, a younger man, appeared and told von Werra he'd take him along the line to the station.

As they trudged along the line, the young fireman fired questions at him asking him where he had come from, how he managed to crash and so on. With growing confidence, von Werra answered them and the fireman seemed satisfied with his story. It was not until well after 5 a.m. that they arrived at a signal box where the fireman passed him over to the signalman. Once more he repeated his story to the man urging him to get him to a telephone quickly but the signalman pointed out that the only phone available was one in the booking office which did not open till six. He would have to wait.

Just before six o'clock Mr. Sam Eaton, the booking

clerk arrived to go on duty but since there was a train due shortly he did not immediately have time to deal with von Werra and asked him to be patient. At last, with the rush over, he turned his attentions to the German. Von Werra went through the story once more, imagining that he would have the 'easy ride' he had had with the train driver and the fireman but Sam Eaton was a different kettle of fish. He fired questions at von Werra at such speed that it left the 'Dutchman' almost breathless. Sam Eaton took the warnings about 'Spies in Your Midst' seriously and he was taking no chances.

In between bouts of questioning von Werra pressed Mr Eaton to allow him to phone the nearest aerodrome. Perhaps it was because the 'Dutchman' was just a bit too forthcoming with details of the raid he had been on that Sam Eaton decided not to ring the aerodrome but to phone the *police* instead. This decision stunned von Werra. He hadn't counted on the police being called in. He was worried and asked Sam Eaton why he could not get directly in touch with the aerodrome.

'Just a formality,' Eaton assured him but it was more than that. There were nagging doubts in Sam Eaton's mind. He'd heard nothing of a crash and something about the 'Dutchman's' story just didn't ring true. He got von Werra to write his name and unit down on a piece of paper and he relayed that to the policeman who answered the phone. After a lengthy conversation he hung up. 'They'll be along any minute,' he told von Werra. The 'Dutchman' was by then decidedly edgy. The last thing he wanted was a confrontation with the police and he urged Sam Eaton to put through a call to Hucknall, which he had discovered was the nearest R.A.F. station. After yet another barrage of questions, Eaton relented and rang the base where he was passed from one person to another until at last he was put through to the duty officer who in turn asked a whole series of questions about the mysterious Captain van Lott. In desperation, having by then repeated the story von Werra had told him several times, Sam Eaton handed the receiver to von Werra and told him to explain the position himself.

Von Werra launched himself into the fabricated story yet again, sticking firmly to the facts he had concocted. After another barrage of questions, the duty officer to whom he was speaking finally agreed to send transport to pick him up. With that the conversation ended. Von Werra prayed that his transport would come before the police arrived, saving a lot of explanation.

Not long after, however, the door opened and in walked three men, two dressed in civilian clothes and the other in the uniform of a police sergeant. Von Werra was taken aback when he saw the plain-clothes men. He hadn't bargained for being confronted with what he thought was the British equivalent of the Gestapo. (In fact they were two plain-clothes police detectives.) Wild rumours had been spread throughout Germany by the propaganda machine telling of the cruelty of the British 'Gestapo'. Now he thought he was in for a taste of their methods. Once more van Lott went through his story but this time the questions fired at him were more cunning. Somehow the 'Dutchman' managed to battle through them with some degree of conviction. He was getting decidedly hot under the collar. The questioning went on at some length until finally the three policemen seemed satisfied with his story. They bade him farewell and they left. Minutes later an R.A.F. airman arrived with a car to take him to the aerodrome.

Von Werra breathed a sigh of relief. The ordeal he had just undergone had taxed his nerves and it was a blessed relief to climb into the car and relax on the drive towards Hucknall. But had he known it then, he had little cause to feel that things were going well for him.

The duty officer had not been fooled by van Lott's story and indeed the only reason transport had been sent for him was not to rescue a crashed bomber pilot in distress but to get von Werra on the camp where they could keep an eye on him and confirm that he was in fact bogus.

The car swept in through the camp gates and towards the Station Headquarters building. As it did so, von Werra took particular note of the aircraft parked outside the hangars. He asked the driver what type of airfield it was and got quite a shock when he was told that it was a Service Training School for *Polish* pilots. The reason this gave von Werra a jolt was simple. The Poles had a bitter hatred of the Germans after all they had suffered during the invasion and von Werra knew only too well that he would receive no mercy if he fell into the hands of the Poles. He also learned that although one half of the airfield was operated by the R.A.F., the other at the far side from where he was, was used by Rolls Royce and was strictly 'hush-hush' where only authorised R.A.F. personnel were allowed.

Soon they arrived at Station Headquarters and von Werra was shown into the adjutant's office where he was confronted by the duty officer who invited him to take off his flying suit and relax, but this was the one thing von Werra did not want to do for he wore no uniform underneath. He succeeded in stalling the duty officer by making a casual excuse then the R.A.F. officer sat down and they went through the story once more. For von Werra the tension was agonising. This was one man he could obviously not fool easily. Then the inevitable happened. The duty officer, trying as best he could to appear offhand, told von Werra that he would, as a matter of routine, have to get in touch with Dyce aerodrome and confirm his story. If von Werra was to get to an aircraft, he had to do it now. The game would be up when Dyce did not confirm his story. The duty officer lifted a telephone receiver and put through the call. Von Werra's mind raced, trying desperately to think of an excuse for leaving the room.

The duty officer was having difficulty in getting through to Dyce but eventually he did. Meanwhile as a matter of formality, he asked to see von Werra's identity disc. Von Werra willingly agreed and put his hand inside his flying suit to retrieve it but as his hand found it, he almost gasped in horror. Far from being the neat, oblong disc which had been carefully manufactured in the prisoner-of-war camp, it had been transformed into distorted pulp by the heat from his body. To show it to the duty officer would mean instant discovery as an impostor. But providence was on his side. As he was fumbling in his flying suit, Dyce came on the line and the duty officer's attention was diverted for the moment. Now was the time to get out, and fast.

Von Werra got up from his seat and gestured to the British officer that he was going to the toilet then slipped out of the room. He could hear the duty officer talking, obviously on a bad line to Dyce, as he walked unnoticed out of the main door of Station Headquarters.

It was still early morning and the station had not yet come to life so he took a chance and ran along the road, away from headquarters towards some hangars in the distance. He had to find an aircraft fast before the balloon went up. He made his way nearer to the hangars slowing down as he did so. He could see some people ahead but most important of all, a group of Hurricane fighters. He had reached the civilian side of the aerodrome. If only he could lay his hands on one of these fighters, he thought, he could be off in no time. What a triumph he thought, to escape from England and bring back to Germany a brand new Hurricane fighter. But he had to dispel this possibility from his mind for the time being. He hadn't got his fighter yet. Then he noticed that one of the fighters had an accumulator trolley sitting beside it. That meant only one thing—it was about to be started up. What better chance would he have? Nearby the same fighter was a mechanic and von Werra walked boldly towards him and greeted him with a friendly 'Good morning'.

Von Werra's genius for the inventive came into play now when he explained that he had just been posted to the base and had been sent over to make a practice flight in a Hurricane, since he had not yet flown one. The mechanic could not understand this because his company was a civilian one and had no dealings with the R.A.F.

'But this is urgent,' von Werra explained. It was urgent all right.

It was the mechanic himself who unwittingly furnished von Werra with his excuse when it dawned on him that Captain van Lott must be a ferry pilot. Von Werra accepted the mechanic's interpretation and asked him if he could now get on with looking at the controls. The mechanic said he would first have to sign the visitors' book and went off to fetch the manager. After a few minutes, the manager himself arrived and told von Werra it would be necessary for him to complete the required documents before being allowed to fly a Hurricane. Impatiently, von Werra followed the man into a building where he filled in the details as best he could in a large book, entering his fictitious identity. Then with that completed, he was taken back out to the Hurricane.

It stood there gleaming in the early morning sun—waiting for him. He was only minutes away from success now but every second counted. The mechanic jumped up on the wing and slid open the canopy. Von Werra followed and dropped into the cockpit. He stared in disbelief at the instruments in front of him. He was baffled. The instruments bore little resemblance to those he'd used in his Messerschmitt. The mechanic went through the instruments explaining what they each were, but von Werra's main concern was getting the Hurricane started and into the air. He'd worry about the rest when he was airborne. He pressed the starter button but a yell from the mechanic stopped him. He could not start the aircraft without an accumulator trolley and the one that had been sitting beside the aircraft had gone. Von Werra was furious but hid his anger and asked the mechanic to get one quickly. Von Werra drummed his fingers anxiously on the control column in front of him as the mechanic made off to find the trolley. By then he was trembling with expectation. If only he'd hurry, von Werra thought, then he felt someone climb up on to the wing. At last ... but as he turned his head to see the mechanic, he stared right into the muzzle of a revolver. The hand that held it was that of the duty officer.

'Get out!' he ordered. For von Werra, the game was up and with a heavy heart he slowly climbed out of the cockpit and was led away to captivity. He cursed his luck. He had got so near; so close to pulling off his escape bid, only to be foiled at the last minute because someone had moved an accumulator trolley.

Back in Station Headquarters, he admitted his identity to the station adjutant. Pretence was useless and he resigned himself to the fact that he was 'in the bag' once more.

The very fact that von Werra had succeeded in getting as far as he had was no mean achievement in itself and as a result of it no fewer than five full-scale enquiries were held to find out how he had done it and who was to blame for him getting that far.

Von Werra was duly returned to imprisonment under close guard in Swanwick cage but not long after his arrival, he received some disturbing news. He, along with many others, was to be transferred to another camp ... but this one was to be in *Canada*!

For many German prisoners whose minds were bent on escape, the prospect of internment in Canada was the end of the line. Escape from Britain was a difficult enough proposition with the problem of getting across the English Channel but how could they possibly make it across the Atlantic? For von Werra, this merely offered fresh opportunities for escape. Indeed, he thought, escape might be even easier! After all, he reasoned, the United States of America was not at that time involved in the war and as a neutral country he could find refuge there. After he had considered these fresh developments he was far from downhearted. In fact he was elated at the prospect of another attempt to escape.

Throughout the long transatlantic voyage, von Werra learned all he could about Canada from Leutnant Wagner who had lived in that country before the war. Von Werra pestered Wagner daily finding out all he could about the people and the geography of the country and he actually had Wagner draw him a map of the Canadian/American border from memory so that he could plan his escape more accurately.

Never one to miss an opportunity, von Werra even considered the possibility of capturing the ship in which they were being transported across the Atlantic and taking it to Germany but this suggestion had to be discounted because of the heavily-armed warship which escorted them and which could with ease blow them clean out of the water.

At last their ship arrived in Canada and docked at Halifax where von Werra and the others were shepherded on to a closely guarded train bound for a prisoner-of-war camp on the north shore of Lake Ontario, in the depths of Canada. They were hustled into a long, comfortable carriage where they were each allotted a seat. Von Werra, Manhard, Wagner and Wilhelm found themselves sitting together with von Werra next to the double set of windows ... just the position he had wanted. If he was going to make a bid for escape, what better time, he thought, than during the journey to the camp. This was particularly good since, as Wagner explained, the train would in all probability take a route along the frontier for part of its journey.

No sooner had the train pulled out of Halifax than von Werra was working out a plan of escape. His only hope of getting out of the train was through the double set of windows by which he sat but he found that although he could open the inside window with ease, the one on the outside was frozen solid by the icy blast of the Canadian winter. While his companions kept a weather eye on the ever-watchful guards who patrolled the carriages, von Werra, screened by a blanket which he had wrapped around himself, worked on the outside window. The journey was to last several days and it was not until the train had reached a point east of Montreal that von Werra succeeded in edging the outside window open and wedging it there. The escape bid had to come soon to avoid discovery.

On the night that the train pulled out of Montreal, von Werra decided to strike. Clad in a thick coat, given him before he left England, he pretended to huddle in sleep by the window. Then, as arranged, he edged up the inner window without the guards noticing. Minutes later, as everyone was settling down, Wagner stood up and shook his blanket, an apparently casual move before retiring for the night. But as he did so, the blanket screened von Werra from the guard and the German grabbed his chance. In one deft move, he heaved open the outer window and dived headlong out into the deep snow by the track while one of his companions slammed the window closed behind him and the three remaining men sat down in their seats as if nothing had happened.

Von Werra lay half-dazed in the snow watching the

lights of the train retreating into the distance. His whole body seemed to ache from the impact of the fall but luckily he had not broken any bones. Instantly the freezing cold overtook him and he clambered to his feet. He had to move on or he would freeze to death where he stood. He trudged off southwards through the snow until he came to a dense forest which lay in his path south. He battled his way through the closely knit trees until, after hours of trudging through the snow, he reached a roadway and walked along it for some miles, stumbling with exhaustion as he went. At length he reached the north bank of the mighty St Lawrence river, the last barrier between him and freedom in the United States. Luck was with him because at that time of year the St Lawrence was frozen over, thick with ice.

Across the vast expanse of ice, von Werra could see the lights of a town and he headed off over the rough frozen surface towards it. Every step he took seemed to sap the energy from him. He had been on the go for almost twenty-four hours without a break and he was near the point of utter exhaustion. His head reeled but he fought on over the ice until, half crawling, he stopped. He had met what he thought was the ultimate barrier—a point where the river had not frozen and there was an impassable fast-flowing river of ice-cold water. Swimming it was out of the question. He would be killed instantly by the freezing cold water. With a heavy heart he struggled back over the ice to the Canadian bank of the river. It seemed that he had been pipped at the post but as he got back to the shore he noticed a strange, even hump in the snow. Clearing the covering of snow away he found a boat. If only he could get the boat across the ice to the river he would still have a chance of making it to America. Summoning all his strength he managed to free the boat from the grip of the ice and dragged it on to the frozen river, then he got behind it and began to push.

The effort of pushing the boat taxed every ounce of the little remaining energy he had but after a marathon push over the ice he reached the water. He edged the boat into the water and clambered aboard. Without oars he was powerless to steer the boat and it floated with the current until it bumped up against the ice on the other side. Von Werra pulled himself out of the boat and half collapsed on to the snow but he managed to struggle to his feet once more. He was covered from head to toe in snow and his ears were severely frost-bitten. He made his way inland still not sure that he was in the United States because Wagner had warned him that at some points, both banks of the St Lawrence are in Canada. Stumbling on through the night he at last came to a road where he saw a car with two people standing by it.

Swaying as he went and on the point of collapse, he rocked towards the two people, whose car had broken down. Before saying a word to the two people who gazed in surprise at the apparition which had emerged from the night, he looked at the number plate on the car. On it were written the words 'New York' ... he had made it. He was free.

But von Werra's troubles were far from over. He was arrested by the United States police and technically charged with vagrancy and illegal entry before being handed over to the German Embassy in New York. Overnight he had become headline news in the United States. His escape brought banner headlines. But there were those who were considering a request by the Canadian government for his extradition—back into the bag. Von Werra, however, was not prepared to hang around and wait for a decision. One night, he disappeared from the German Embassy and 'escaped' over the border into South America.

In due course von Werra made his way back to Germany via Mexico, Panama, Peru, Bolivia and the Argentine, before finally crossing the Atlantic to West Africa then on to Spain and Rome before flying back to Germany. Von Werra returned to a hero's welcome and national acclaim.

To the Allies the loss of one man from a prisoner-of-war camp was, on the face of it, of little consequence but von Werra's return to Germany was to have serious consequences. He was no sooner back in the Fatherland than he got to work writing down his experiences in detail, notably those he had encountered under interrogation. This was the most important feature of his escape. No longer would the British interrogators be able subtly to extract information from captured Germans. Von Werra 'spilled the beans' about the techniques the British were employing and as a result of this, German army, navy and air force personnel were given strict orders about how to conduct themselves when being interrogated by the British. In his way, von Werra struck a more deadly blow at the British on the ground than he ever did in the air.

Furthermore, his escape had a significant effect upon Allied prisoners of war in German camps. Von Werra toured their camps advising the commandants on how to tighten up security and even paid a visit to the notorious Colditz Castle which resulted in a severe tightening up there.

For a while, von Werra continued in his role as adviser to the camp commandants but he was anxious to get back to action where the real glory was. He was transferred to a fighter unit and on 25 October, 1941, his aircraft crashed into the sea off the Dutch coast. Franz von Werra, the intrepid German escaper, was dead. Had he not been quite so successful as an escaper, he might well have been alive today to tell his own story.

# 4

# *Jungle Break*

The scorching sun burned through the skulls and tortured the brains of the near-delirious crowd of ragged men who stood in uneven rows in the Pasir Panjang compound, on the island of Singapore. They had been there since dawn and now it was almost four o'clock in the afternoon. Already many of them had succumbed to collapse but this had been the signal for their Japanese captors to pounce, wielding rifle butts and clubbing the prostrate figures until, battered senseless, they were hauled to their feet.

At precisely five o'clock, a Japanese sergeant strode between the lines of men, his narrow eyes sizing up each of them as he passed. At intervals he stopped in his tracks and pointed to one of the taller men in the ranks, who was then hustled out of the line at bayonet point to wait in front of the crowd of men. He chose eleven men, all of them Australians but barely recognisable as such in their torn clothes. Even in their half bent, emaciated state they towered over their squat, thick-set Japanese guards.

Each of the eleven men had his hands tied behind his back and was made to stand there before the assembled prisoners. Few of the men who remained in the crowd lifted their eyes to watch ... they knew what was coming.

At an order hissed from the sergeant, a group of Japanese guards marched purposefully towards the eleven men with their bayonets levelled, then thrust the lengths of steel into the stomachs of the trussed-up men. One by one the Australians fell to the ground, their bellies ripped open by the blades. Blood poured from their wounds drenching the dusty brown soil. Their murderers continued the slaughter with expressionless faces and marched among their writhing victims jabbing them in the throat with their bayonets until the last vestige of life was jerked out of their bodies.

As the groans and screams of the Australians died away, the mass of prisoners began to surge forward, infuriated at the horror they had just witnessed and bent on revenge. But as they did so, a Japanese guard swung his machine-gun on to them and squeezed the trigger, raking the crowd with bullets. Three men dropped to the ground, cut down by the fusilade of fire. At that the crowd of men halted. Vengeance was futile.

For a moment the tension was electric, everyone waiting for the other to make a move, then a young Australian lieutenant stepped out in front of the men and begged them to calm down. The men shuffled back into line once more and the lieutenant, summoning all his strength and courage, marched over to the Japanese officer who had stood watching the whole hellish carnage without showing the slightest emotion. The Australian pointed out as forcibly as he could that the Japanese had committed a heinous crime and violated the code of war. The Japanese officer made no reply but simply motioned to a guard who smashed the lieutenant in the spine with the butt of his rifle, then he was dragged off by two guards. As he was hauled across the ground, the lieutenant half turned his dropping head towards the watching crowd of prisoners and yelled:

'Mark these bastards for future reference!'

He was never seen again.

Sergeant Charles McCormac, R.A.F., was one of those who witnessed the slaughter. He was bewildered, unable to believe what he had just seen. He knew the Japanese to be ruthless killers with a totally different code of war and he had already tasted their brutality, but the bloody sight that lay before him was almost too much to comprehend and his empty stomach heaved but was unable to react to the sickening nausea that swept through him.

The words of the Japanese commandant were still ringing in McCormac's ears. He remembered the warning he and all the other prisoners had received when they were bundled into the remote prison camp, deep in the heart of a banana plantation. 'There will be no escape!' he had said. But some men had tried and got through the wire. None of them was ever heard of again. Whether they had succeeded in evading the Japanese guards, McCormac did not know but the commandant had promised reprisals and the massacre he had seen was just that. There could not possibly have been a more potent deterrent to escape than the one McCormac had just witnessed. But in spite of the horror, men were to make a break for it ... and McCormac was to be one of them.

McCormac, perhaps more than many others in that compound, had good reason to escape. He had been accused of being a spy—and the Japs had special methods of dealing with spies. Rumours were rife in the camp about the fate that befell those who were involved in spying. The Japanese had perfected the art of the slow death and one of their specialities was to tie a man spread-eagled over young bamboo shoots and leave him there. The bamboo shoots grew some five inches a day and could penetrate flesh with ease. The result of such a terrible torture need hardly be described. All the Japs required to subject a man to this agonising death was to *believe* he was a spy—they needed no firm proof. This was what most certainly lay in store for McCormac. The tragedy was that McCormac was no spy then and never had been.

Charles McCormac was born in 1915, the son of a planter who managed a plantation in Malaya and during his childhood days there he learned to speak Malay fluently with a working knowledge of Chinese, Tamil and Japanese, something which many years later was to prove the difference between life and death for him. He was sent to school in Australia and at the age of eighteen joined the R.A.F. as a wireless-operator technician. After training for aircrew duties, he was posted to a squadron in Malaya, operating in flying-boats. At the age of twenty-five, he married a Eurasian girl and they settled down in married quarters in Singapore.

Life was good for McCormac. He had a beautiful wife, a job he enjoyed doing and a pleasant home. Having spent most of his life in Malaya, he had grown to know and love the people, learning of their ways and customs. All in all, fate had been kind to him but it was not to last. Japan declared war and soon the Yellow Peril was sweeping down the Malay Peninsula. Singapore was protected only for a sea-borne attack. The defenders had not envisaged an army attacking them from any other direction. After all, Malaya was almost all dense jungle which they regarded as impenetratable by an army of any size. Tragically they were to be proved wrong. The Japanese were experts in the art of jungle warfare and they moved with startling rapidity down the Malay Peninsula and in one bloody battle, captured Singapore.

The fall of the island, Britain's most important sea base in the Far East, came as a shocking blow and Britain was stunned at the ease with which the Japanese had taken the island. That is not to say that those who defended the island did not put up a determined fight; they did, but the weight of Japanese numbers quickly overcame their determination and to avoid untold slaughter they had to surrender. Among those who put up such a valiant defence of the island was McCormac who first ensured that his wife, Pat, was evacuated on one of the last ships to leave the island before the Japanese arrived. His concern for his wife's safety was well-founded for he knew only too well that the Japanese dealt ruthlessly with Eurasian girls. They, like the Germans with the Jews, regarded Eurasians as 'impure' and worthy only of death —generally a slow and torturous one.

Having got Pat safely off on the boat, McCormac returned to his home, took off his R.A.F. uniform and donned fresh and clean civilian clothes. The fact that he changed clothes was to have terrible consequences for him, but at the time his one thought was to freshen up then launch himself into the fray to defend his beloved island. He joined up with a group of volunteer fighters who put up a determined and bitter fight against the Japs swarming through the streets, wiping out all that lay in their path. Resistance soon began to crumble as more of the enemy swept across the island and eventually McCormac was captured.

The Japs accused McCormac of spying and sabotage. They made their excuse for the accusation the white shirt he was wearing. Had he been in the R.A.F. as he had claimed then he would have been in uniform. In spite of his protests to the contrary, the Japanese refused to believe him and the more he said the more deeply entrenched the Japs became in their belief. McCormac was to be singled out for 'special treatment' when the time came. He, along with hundreds of other prisoners, was thrown into the hastily improvised prisoner-of-war camp in the remote region of Pasir Panjang.

The camp was a crude affair, consisting of a ring of barbed wire and bamboo strung around a clearing no more than one hundred yards square in the midst of a banana plantation. The Japs were not a party to the Geneva Convention and therefore pleased themselves about how the prisoners of war should be treated. The compound was crammed with hundreds of British and Australian servicemen as well as civilians who had hardly sufficient room to move and were denied the basic necessities of life. Their food consisted of a tiny handful of rice and a strip of dried fish served once a day. On this pitiful diet, the prisoners were not only supposed to survive but also do a hard day's work. Every day groups of men were marched off to the docks where they were employed on back-breaking work. They were worked from dawn till dusk in the burning heat. None of them had been used to such exertion under such conditions and quickly succumbed to disease. In no time at all their bodies became emaciated and dysentery quickly took its toll, sometimes before a Japanese bayonet could 'dispose of' the useless ones who could not work. The men crowded into that compound were subjected to the most horrible privations by their captors who regarded them with contempt and worth less than cattle.

Such then were the conditions which existed in the camp and a few determined men made their attempts to escape. All had failed and their failure had resulted in the slaughter which was described earlier. An attempt to escape was tantamount to a death sentence for one's comrades and this alone dissuaded others from making the break. It was clear that the Japanese relied on this threat as a deterrent since the compound in which the prisoners were kept was extremely primitive, the barbed wire being intended only as an indication of the camp limits rather than a means of keeping them captive.

There was one other major deterrent upon which the Japanese relied and that was the jungle itself with all the dangers it held, the most notable of which were the poisonous snakes. The most feared of all these venomous creatures was the deadly krait, a comparatively small snake, about eighteen inches in length, which attacked the eyes. Its bite meant instantaneous death. There were other perils that lurked in the dense and often dark jungle, like pythons, poisonous spiders, scorpions and wild boars which would attack a man. All this formed a natural barrier between the captives and freedom. Few of them knew the jungle well enough to survive in it. If they did not die at the hands of the Japs, the would-be escapers would inevitably succumb to death in the jungle. McCormac knew the jungle and he knew the dangers that lurked within it. He was no stranger to it but he appreciated that it could be a friend as well as an enemy.

With the certainty of horrible death hanging over his head, the prospect of escape was continually in McCormac's thoughts. Staying where he was meant waiting for a slow and agonising death whereas at large in the jungle he knew at least he would have a fighting chance. But how does a man reconcile saving his own skin with inevitably sentencing some of his comrades to death in doing so? The thought plagued him until, the day after the executions had taken place, he was taken to the Y.M.C.A. building in the town of Pasir Panjang. There he was pushed into a room and he came face to face with one of the most evil men in the Imperial Japanese Army ... a Japanese officer named Teruchi. This vile creature was a senior officer of the infamous *Kempei-Tai*, the Japanese 'thought police'. His speciality was interrogation and he was a master of the art. Unlike his counterparts in the German Gestapo, there was no attempt at subtlety in his techniques. Brutality of the most horrific kind was the password to successful interrogation with the *Kempei-Tai* and they had evolved methods which do not bear recounting. Suffice to say that, by comparison, the methods employed by the Gestapo were 'humane'.

McCormac sensed immediately that Teruchi seemed to radiate evil. He was short and squat with broad, heavy shoulders, obviously a powerful man and one who was used to using that power.

Speaking in English with a strong American accent, he launched into McCormac with a barrage of questions, accusing him all the time of being a spy, in spite of McCormac's protests to the contrary. As the questions continued and McCormac continued to deny he was a spy, the Jap's temper rose until he could restrain himself no longer and kicked the Englishman in the stomach with his heavy boot. Still McCormac protested his innocence only to be booted again and again. By then he had fallen to his knees and continued to be on the receiving end of the Jap's kicks. Pain racked his body as the blows thudded into him. Then Teruchi changed his approach, questioning him about his wife and her whereabouts.

McCormac told the Jap his wife had been evacuated by ship and was on her way to England. At least, McCormac thought, they could not get at her but the Jap half grinned.

'Ah, yes.' Teruchi leered. 'On the *Wakefield*. She was sunk by one of our ships and there were no survivors. Your wife is dead!'

A surge of emotion came over the beaten McCormac. His whole life seemed to collapse around him. But how could he be sure that the Jap was telling the truth? Could this not just be an attempt to break him? He tried to console himself with that thought as Teruchi turned to interrogating him about the whereabouts of his wife's family. McCormac knew only too well what fate would befall them if he were to reveal their whereabouts.

Teruchi's temper grew as McCormac refused to tell him what he wanted and at last the Jap drew his long Samurai sword from its scabbard and waved its point in his prisoner's face. Teruchi jabbed the point of the sword into McCormac's face and it slit the skin alongside his eye. Blood trickled down his cheek from the wound and Teruchi jabbed again, this time slitting the skin alongside his mouth as McCormac ducked defensively. Now his face was streaming with blood. Teruchi seemed satisfied with his handiwork for the time being and with a parting warning that they would meet again in the very near future, he ordered the guards to take McCormac away.

With that, the battered, bruised and bleeding McCormac was bundled out of the building and frogmarched back to the compound, four miles away, where he was thrown bodily through the gate. One of the prisoners, an Australian called Donaldson, hurried as best he could to where McCormac lay bleeding on the ground. He was much older than McCormac and not a military man. He, like the others, had that gaunt expression that all the prisoners shared. Lack of proper food had transformed this once robust businessman into a walking shadow of his former self. In spite of his weak frame, Donaldson summoned the strength to haul McCormac to his feet and helped him away from the gate. He laid the injured man on the ground then ministered to his wounds as best he could, using the only thing available to clean the gashes on McCormac's face, pieces of dirty cloth torn from McCormac's shirt.

While Donaldson tended to his wounds, McCormac told him what had happened and explained the inevitability of his fate. Death, it seemed, was an imminent certainty for him. Escape was possible but the horrific consequences for his comrades forced him to discount it. He knew only too well that if he made a break for it from his working party, all the others would be executed in reprisal.

It was not until the next day that Donaldson came up

with an idea while they were being marched down to the docks. Why, he reasoned, could not the entire working party escape. That way the Japs wouldn't have anybody to execute. For the first time, McCormac felt a faint ray of hope. But before getting too excited at the prospect they had to check with the others in their work party to determine if they were willing to take the risk. The result came as a blow to them. None of the others was interested. Some thought they'd never make it while others were prepared to sit it out and wait for the Allies to recapture Singapore. It seemed as if their hopes of ever getting free of that hell had been dashed for ever. But luck was to be on their side. They found a friend on the outside.

Although they were guarded when they went on their daily working parties to the docks, the 'gang-boss' was not a Japanese but a Portuguese Eurasian. Outwardly he sympathised with the Japanese but in truth his sympathy was born of fear not for himself but for his family. He had good reason to hate the Japs. They had taken his elder daughter from his home and raped her. He had not seen her since. For the sake of his wife and family he could not outwardly defy the Japs but he could do it secretly and he was willing to take the risk. His name was Rodriguez and one day he approached McCormac and asked him bluntly why he did not attempt to escape. McCormac was taken aback at the suggestion coming out of the blue and was at first wary of this seemingly unwarranted gesture of friendliness. But when he heard Rodriguez's story, he knew that he had found a man he could trust.

The Eurasian told McCormac and Donaldson he had a brother who was at that very time in the hills of Malaya with a band of guerrillas fighting the Japanese. He knew also of a boat which could take them across the Jahore Straits to the mainland. Once there they could join up with his brother's guerrillas who were hidden out in the heart of Malaya at Kuala Lipis.

The offer seemed too good to be true and now with renewed heart they reconsidered their plight but the same old problems arose—the fate of their comrades if they made a break. It was Donaldson who hit on a new idea. Why not, he suggested, recruit men from other working parties who were willing to make a break and swop them with those who were reluctant in their own party. That way the entire party would make a break for it and they would overcome the problem of reprisals. After all, he explained, the Japs only took a head count when the working party went to the docks. There was no roll call so it didn't matter who went along on the parties so long as there was the requisite number of men. It might, they thought, just work.

That night, they scoured the camp for volunteers and soon found the required number of men willing to make the break with them. The following morning the swop was made and a new party marched off to the docks.

While the Jap guards were not looking, McCormac and Donaldson talked in whispers to Rodriguez who willingly offered his help once more, although his willingness was tempered with a degree of caution.

'I'll do all I can to help,' he told them, 'as long as you don't make the break during the day while you're with me. You'll have to break out at night then make your way to my house at Paya Lebar. I'll take you to the boat from there.'

'Agreed. We'll fix up a plan of escape when we get back to camp and let you know tomorrow when the break's going to be. Okay?'

With that they got back to work and when they returned to the camp that night McCormac and the others set about devising a plan. Huddled together, ever watchful of the guards, they formulated their plan of action.

The compound was well lit at night by high-powered lamps along the barbed wire entanglement and they reasoned that before they could make their attempt they would have to deal with the lights. The tropical night came quickly to Singapore, usually around six-thirty. If they could fix things so that the lights failed to work when night came, they could rush to the flimsy gate, break it down and then scatter into the surrounding plantation and jungle. The most important factor in the whole operation would be speed. The element of surprise was vital to catch the Japs off guard. The slightest hesitation would mean certain death for all concerned.

McCormac knew where the junction box for the electricity supply was to be found. It was conveniently placed just outside the wire and he volunteered to pull the leads just before the break-out. The plan was agreed and the men returned to their personal patches of ground where they settled down to an uneasy sleep.

The following day, the tension among the men who were marched off to the docks was electric. McCormac was troubled. All it needed now was for him to be summoned by Teruchi to ruin his plans. He tried to cast the thought from his mind but without success. He and Donaldson whispered their plan to Rodriguez who gave them directions to his house. He would be ready and waiting for them. The day passed agonisingly slowly until, at last, the Jap guard ordered them to stop work and marched them back to camp.

At 6.15 p.m., as the hot sun was sinking beneath the horizon, McCormac and his group of patriots sidled over towards the wire as inconspicuously as they could. McCormac crouched by the wire, shielded from a nearby guard by the group of men. He flattened himself on the ground and stretched his arm through the wire to tug at two of the leads on the junction box. They came away easily in his hand and he scrambled to his feet and continued chatting to the others as if nothing had happened.

Gradually they shuffled over towards the gate, taking great care not to act suspiciously. Then as the last rays of light disappeared, they saw a Jap guard march over to a small hut where the light switches were housed. He entered through the open door then seconds later the whole hut erupted in a violent explosion shaking the entire compound.

'Jesus Christ—it's blown up!' one of them yelled.

For a moment they stood riveted to the spot until Donaldson gelled into action ...

'Now!' he screeched and the group of men dashed to the gate and barged through it.

In an instant the compound was swarming with guards. Rifle shots rang out as they spotted the men darting out of the gate.

Japs poured out of the guard hut just outside the gate and in front of the escapers then loosed off a few rounds at them but the prisoners charged headlong into the soldiers. Each of them had with him a makeshift weapon and they hacked and clubbed at the guards with them.

Donaldson wielded a home-made lead cosh with which he clubbed one of the guards. Summoning all his strength, he brought the cosh down on the guard's head and the heavy lead weight sank into the Jap's skull so deeply that Donaldson could not get it free again. Furious, he pulled the Jap's bayonet from its scabbard and left the cosh impaled in the skull.

Meanwhile, McCormac launched an attack on a squat little Jap, battering him senseless about the head with a lump of wood, then he too grabbed the guard's bayonet and darted off into the banana trees with bullets whipping through the air dangerously close to him. While he scrambled through the trees, he could hear the hell of the battle that raged behind him but he crashed on and as he did so he was aware of someone else rushing through the trees behind him. It was Donaldson. Both men swept on through the trees for some minutes before they stopped to catch their breath. By then the noise of rifle and machine-gun fire had died slightly and they slowed to a walk.

Sweat streamed off their sinewy bodies and their hearts thumped. They were near to dropping but they had to force themselves on through the plantation. Search parties would be hot on their heels and if they were to pull off their escape they had to keep going or all would be lost. As they continued through the forest of trees they pondered on the fate of their friends. Some of them must have been caught in the hail of bullets put up by the Japs—but how many, they wondered.

On they went, breathlessly plodding through the tall grass and trees. There was a long way to go before they reached their destination but soon they came to the edge of the plantation. Then was the time for extreme caution. They crouched low as they made their way across country, skirting the perimeter of Singapore town. The night began to play tricks on their senses and every shadow took on the shape of a Jap soldier crouched, ready to loose off a hail of bullets at them.

For three hours they trekked on until they reached a huge tree which Rodriguez had told them was only yards from his house. They crept towards it then suddenly they stopped in their tracks. They heard the rustle of grass nearby. Japs, they thought. They stayed motionless until two figures emerged from the dark shadows and they recognised them as two more of the escapers. In hurried whispers they identified themselves.

They stayed where they were with the tension almost killing. The four men huddled together, visibly trembling with excitement and the strain of their dash for freedom.

Then more rustles were heard in the grass and one by one more of their friends joined them. They waited for fifteen minutes hoping that the others would arrive but there was no sign of them and they could wait no longer. McCormac, anxious to get on, slipped out of cover into the shadow of Rodriguez's house and knocked on the door. Seconds later, the Eurasian appeared. He was obviously terrified. The alarm had been raised and Japs were everywhere, scouring the town for escapers. McCormac saw the frightened state of the man and was stunned when Rodriguez told him he could not take them to the boat. Hurriedly, he told McCormac where the boat was to be found, lying on the mud-flats at Kranji Point. Then he shoved a wad of paper money into the Englishman's hand and disappeared behind the door. McCormac understood the man's reluctance to help. He obviously feared for the safety of his wife and children if he were caught.

Stuffing the money into his pocket, McCormac made off back to where Donaldson and the others were waiting and moving as quickly as they could they headed off in the direction of Kranji Point. To lessen the chances of all being caught together they split up into twos and threes, keeping well apart. They carried on like this through the night until, by some miracle of navigation, McCormac led them on to the mud-flats. But they had taken only a few steps on to the mud when they spotted some dark shadows moving not twenty yards from where they were. They were Japs and they had been seen.

The still night was instantly shattered by the sound of explosions as the Japs opened up on the escapers.

'Get the bastards!' someone yelled, and *en masse* they charged at the Japs.

McCormac lunged at one of them, heedless of the rifle that was pointed at him and he slashed at the little Jap with his bayonet, plunging the pointed steel deep into the Jap's body again and again until he slumped lifeless to the ground amid a pool of blood. Like a man possessed, McCormac slashed into another Jap and his blade took its toll while the others hacked at them. The battle was short and bloody. It stopped as suddenly as it started. All the Japs were dead save one who had charged off into the jungle. Bodies lay all about them, some were Japs and the others escapers. They were all dead.

The eight escapers who were left lost no time in darting to where the boat lay on the mud-flats. They had no time to waste. Soon the whole area would be crawling with Japs. Anxious hands grabbed at the boat and slid it easily into the water and they bundled in. One of them clutched a paddle which had been left in the boat and paddled with all his might, driving the tiny craft out into the water.

They had to get to the mainland before the hornets' nest was roused and patrol boats came out after them but, when they reached a point barely two hundred yards from the shore, there was a sudden blaze of light from the mud-flats they had just left.

'A searchlight!' one of them cursed. 'Get down.'

The eight men flattened themselves in the boat and waited. The circle of light swept across the oily, calm water then fixed on the boat but passed on again. With thumping hearts they waited for the burst of machine-gun fire that must surely come. But no. The bright pool of light came back again, held for a moment on the boat then swept on over the water. The Japs, they thought, must have reckoned the boat was simply adrift.

Gingerly, McCormac peered over the edge of the gunwales. The searchlight had gone out and he could see by the movement of the lights on the shore that the boat was drifting fast ... out to sea. The tide was carrying them down the strait but that suited them. The farther they could get from Singapore the better.

As the lights on the shore slipped slowly into the distance they were at last able to take stock of the situation. In the boat they found a drum of water, some dried fish and rotten fruit, not enough to last for any length of time but they had to make do.

The night dragged painfully on until at last the first rays of dawn spread out across the sea. They found themselves alone, isolated on a desolate sea. Straining their eyes they could barely make out the thin line of land far off on the horizon. Somehow they had to reach that land or they would eventually perish under the blazing sun, exposed as they were in the little boat. It was then that McCormac hit on the idea of making a sail. There was a small mast in the boat and he gathered together all eight singlets which he intended fashioning into a sail. But as he was setting about his task he happened to glance into the sky and noticed two tiny specks far off in the distance. Aircraft . . . but whose?

Sure enough the small shapes slowly took on the shape of fighters and they were heading steadily in the direction of their boat. They were sweeping low over the water and as they closed in on the boat, one of them shouted:

'Zeros! They're bloody Japs. Get out of the boat!'

Some of the men, McCormac among them, jumped overboard and swam with all their might away from the boat, while others sat where they were, unable to move. They were given the awful choice of dying under a fusillade of bullets or taking their chances with the sharks which lurked in their hundreds beneath the waves in that area.

The fighters roared in on the boat and their machine-guns blazed into life. Bullets zipped into the water, transforming it into a bubbling cauldron, while the others in the boat leapt into the sea and dived underwater. When McCormac surfaced he found the boat upturned and the fighters circling overhead ready to make another run. Down they came twice, more lashing the water and the boat with fire until they turned and zoomed off, obviously content that they had wiped out the occupants.

McCormac surfaced again, gasping for breath. The boat was only a few yards away and he struck out towards it. A head bobbed up nearby. It was Donaldson. Then two more appeared, both of them British soldiers whom McCormac knew only as 'Skinny' and Roy. These were the only others to surface. The rest had fallen either to the Japs' bullets or the sharks.

The four men hauled with all their might on the boat and managed to right it once more but it was filled almost to the gunwales with water. They didn't care; their one thought was to get out of reach of the sharks and they struggled aboard then began bailing out the water.

To their amazement, the boat had sustained relatively little damage. The Jap's cannons had gouged a great hole out of the bows but there were only two neat, small holes below the waterline which McCormac stuffed with cotton from his shirt. After a struggle which sapped away all their remaining strength, they succeeded in getting almost all the water out of the boat and slumped into the well of the vessel, too exhausted to do any more.

Their chief concern was lack of water. They had lost the drum when the boat overturned and now it seemed there was little hope of reaching land. They were at the mercy of the sea and were slowly drifting farther away from the thin strip of land on the horizon. At that time they were too exhausted to care. Day changed into night then fate took a hand and it rained. They lay in the boat cupping their hands to catch the precious drops of fresh water, allowing the rain to soak them through and wringing every droplet out of their soaked clothes.

Dawn came and with it the boiling heat of the sun. Soon they were all almost delirious with thirst and it seemed that the end was near until Skinny spotted something in the sky heading their way. It was an aircraft.

This was it, they thought—the Japs were coming back to finish them off properly.

Then as the aircraft drew nearer, McCormac sat up.

'Hey, that's no fighter ... it's a flying boat!'

All four men sat with their eyes glued to the plane as it soared nearer. Then McCormac's jaw dropped in disbelief as he recognised the type.

'It's not a bloody Jap,' he pointed out. 'It's a Jerry Dornier.'

Skinny was all for giving the boat a wave. Capture by the Germans was preferable to anything the Japs could dish out, he reasoned. But McCormac quickly pointed out that the Germans would merely hand them over to the Japs again. They knew what would become of them then.

The aircraft was droning in on them now and in a final moment of decision, Skinny jumped to his feet and waved frantically to the flying-boat but it merely roared straight overhead and continued on its way.

'Well that settles it,' McCormac said. 'They don't want to know. Maybe it's just as well.'

But the words had hardly left his lips when the huge aircraft swept round in a tight turn and nosed down towards the water. It charged towards the boat then alighted on the water sending up a huge spray as its bows bit into the sea. As it lost speed, it wheeled round and taxied towards the solitary boat. McCormac was tempted to leap into the water and swim away rather than face another session with the Japs but the thought of the sharks waiting for him beneath the waves stopped him.

The flying-boat rode towards them then came to a stop alongside the boat. Moments later a door was shoved open in its side, revealing a young man dressed in white. He offered his hand and Skinny grabbed it and was pulled aboard. The others did likewise and once inside, McCormac collapsed on the floor and began to vomit violently. Between bouts of vomiting, he glanced at the man in white who was joined by another, an oriental. Then something struck him as odd. If they were Germans why weren't they in uniform? He couldn't understand and asked the man in white:

'Who are you?'

'Royal Netherlands Air Force,' he answered.

McCormac lay there stunned, unable to believe what the man had said. They were saved. Of all the miracles, they were saved. By a chance in a million, they had been spotted by the Dutchman. The four survivors were for a moment too amazed to speak, then they burst into excited chatter. Fresh hot cocoa was served to them and they gulped it down thankfully. At last, when the initial excitement had died down and the flying-boat was airborne once more, McCormac managed to gather his bewildered senses and tried to ask some sensible questions.

He gathered from the Dutchman that the flying-boat was heading for a remote swamp in northern Sumatra to pick up refugees. At this, McCormac almost burst with joy for they would be able to link up with British troops there. But his hopes were quickly dashed when the Dutchman explained that Sumatra had been overrun by the Japs. He did point out, however, that the area in which he intended landing was free of the enemy.

'Then can you take us back with you to your base?' McCormac asked.

'Regrettably no,' the Dutchman said sympathetically and explained that he would be carrying a full load as it was and there would be no room for more. They would have to be left in Sumatra to fend for themselves and link up with the guerrillas who were operating in the jungle not far from where he was to drop them. McCormac and the others resigned themselves to this. Their good fortune had already been stretched to the limit.

It was dusk when the flying-boat finally touched down

at its destination and McCormac and his three friends were taken ashore. Later they watched as the flying-boat, crammed to capacity with refugees, swept once more into the night sky, leaving them alone on the edge of the swamp with a wizened old native.

When the flying-boat had finally disappeared from sight, their aged companion led them inland from the stinking swamp until they reached a clearing in the jungle where they found a group of huts mounted on high stilts. Roy was in a particularly bad way, having suffered from severe dysentery for several weeks, which had made him resemble a skeleton with his yellow skin barely covering the bones that protruded in his face. He had to be helped all the way to the native village.

The old man led them to a hut and one by one they struggled up the rickety ladder. Once inside, they were given a meal of rice and water then they lay down and fell into a deep sleep. On the following day the old man returned to the hut and told them that they would have to move on soon as there was a likelihood that the Japanese might pay the village a visit. The penalty for harbouring the enemy would be death for many of the villagers. There was another worry in McCormac's mind. He had heard that a native could earn himself a substantial reward from the Japs for turning over an escapee to them. The temptation for these impoverished peasants must have been great.

McCormac questioned the old man about local guerrillas and where he could find them. They were, the old man assured him, hiding out in the mountains near Lake Toga. This left them with two alternatives. They could strike out for Java which was some 500 miles away or they could head into the mountains and link up with the guerrillas. After due consideration, they decided on the latter. They were all weak and incapable of undertaking a 500-mile trek through the jungle. They would head up into the mountains where they could rest in the comparative cool and re-build their strength before heading for Java.

They stayed at the village for two days during which time they rested and ate well on the hospitality of the natives while McCormac gave his companions lessons on the law of the jungle, its dangers and its advantages. Because of his knowledge of the jungle, McCormac was elected leader of the party and they set off with the farewells of the natives ringing in their ears. Ahead of them lay a six-day trek through the jungle before they were likely to reach the mountains.

For McCormac's three companions the trek that followed was a nightmare. It was almost continuous half-light with the sun obscured by the tall trees and the canopy of leaves over their heads. The heavy, moist atmosphere made breathing difficult and added to the problem of making good progress along the rough, narrow trail they were following. To all of them every dark shadow seemed to hold sudden death. They had visions of deadly poisonous snakes or fierce wild animals lying in wait for them and poised to strike. Both the physical and mental strain were exhausting and they made slow headway.

At night, they struggled up trees and grabbed what sleep they could, wedged between the branches. What little rest they managed to get was tortured by spine-chilling screeches which came from the wild animals roaming the jungle at night. Food was another problem. They had to live off what they could find and their daily diet consisted of a few berries and plant roots, most of which tasted vile and brought on sickness. Roy suffered worst because of his advanced dysentery but he never complained although he must have been constantly in agonising pain. He was wasting away at an alarming rate and had to be helped along by the others.

Fear of running into Japs or Jap sympathisers forced them to avoid a village they found deep in the jungle. There was no way of telling whether or not the villagers might turn them over to the Japs for the reward. The temptation to risk this simply for a decent meal was strong but they had to resist it with all their will-power.

For days they fought their way through the jungle until they reached a rough road. This too held its dangers. A road inevitably meant transport and in all probability it would be Japanese. They lay up by the road for three days, foraging into the jungle for what food and water they could find and during that time they saw many Jap vehicles. Their hide was too dangerous to remain in, so they decided to strike off into the jungle once more but as they did so the ground began to rise and the going became almost impossible. They found no water and little food. Roy was by then in a state of advanced delirium. Their craving for water became so great that they were forced to drink their own urine which made them violently sick. It soon became obvious that their position was hopeless. They would have to return to the road and take their chance at discovering friendly natives.

Back by the road they rested up for yet another three days. Their clothes were in rags, their faces gaunt and covered with stubble giving them the appearance of wild creatures. Roy was getting even worse and it seemed that he would not be able to hold out much longer. The daily diet of berries was doing nothing to help his condition. McCormac did, however, one day stumble upon two dead flying foxes which they stripped of their fur and ate raw. Then McCormac caught a frog which he killed and skinned. They ate it ravenously but shortly after, they were all violently sick.

They could wait by the road no longer and on the fourth day they started off south down the edge of the road, dodging into jungle at the slightest hint of oncoming traffic. At least, they reasoned, they might come across an isolated village where they could get food. They slept by day and walked by night, hoping in that way to avoid stumbling into Japs.

It was not until four wearying days later that they came across a village. But caution had to be observed. There was a good chance that, since the village was on a main road, there would be Japanese there and at dead of night they lay on the perimeter of the village, watching the activity, searching for the slightest hint of Jap occupation. All night they watched while Roy writhed in pain on the ground, groaning almost continuously.

They continued to watch the village closely for most of the following day. But someone had to make a move. They had seen no Japanese but that did not mean that the villagers were not Jap sympathisers. Somebody had to go in there and find out ... and it had to be McCormac. He was the only one who could speak the language.

Drawing a deep breath, McCormac slipped out of their hiding place and walked into the village. He had warned the others that if he was not back within an hour they were to get out of it as quickly as they could.

Donaldson and the others watched as McCormac disappeared amongst the atap huts. He walked boldly up to one large hut and entered to be confronted by several Indonesians and a Chinaman, all sipping coffee. They looked at him as he entered, apparently unconcerned at his arrival. They waited for him to speak.

'Are there any Japanese here?' he asked the Chinaman in the best Chinese he could summon up.

'No, there are no Japanese here,' the Chinaman revealed.

McCormac heaved a sigh of relief and explained that he was not alone. His friends were hidden in the jungle. They were hungry and one of them was sick. The Chinaman questioned him about where he had come from, eyeing him now more suspiciously, or so McCormac thought. Then the Chinaman rose from the ground and left the hut, instructing McCormac to wait.

McCormac was tense with expectation. It might be a trap. The Chinaman could have been bluffing when he said there were no Japs in the village. It might have been a ruse to keep him there while he went to fetch them. All these thoughts ran through McCormac's mind until at last the Chinaman returned with the ageing head man of the village. When McCormac's eyes spotted the medal the old man was wearing he knew he was safe. It was Queen Wilhelmina's Medal and a sure sign that he was friendly. The old man assured McCormac that he was welcome.

McCormac hurried to where his friends lay and brought them into the village where they were given royal treatment. Any enemy of the Japanese was a friend of the villagers. Not long before they had arrived the Japs had come through the village and raped many of their women so there was good cause for the villagers to have a burning hate of them.

Food was plied on them and they ate their first decent meals in weeks, helping to restore their strength. Roy, too, benefited when a native girl used a primitive but effective preparation which cleared up his dysentery. He was like a man who had come back from the dead.

During their stay in the village, they were introduced to a young Chinese called Nang Sen who told them that he would be taking a lorry south and he offered to take them with him. This was what they had hoped for. Their luck, it seemed, was in and later in the day, Nang Sen took them to the most dilapidated lorry they had ever seen, packed with an assortment of goods. He told them to hide under some sheets of rubber and they each squirmed in. Moments later the rickety old machine burst into life and they set off through the night. The lorry bumped and tumbled over the uneven track until as dawn was approaching it stopped in a clearing off the road.

Nang Sen showed them how to obtain water from a certain plant and quinine from another. Then they settled down to sleep for the rest of the day. This pattern continued for the following four days and nights until at last they reached a small village where they rested up for two more days, eating their fill and gradually building up their strength. Then one morning one of the women of the village woke them and bade them follow her. She took the four men to a small boat which was moored by the edge of a river and they scrambled in. The girl rowed the boat downstream until they reached a large village where she pulled the boat up on to the bank then led them off between the huts. At last to their astonishment, they saw a railway track and a stationary freight train with a long line of tarpaulin-covered wagons.

The girl motioned to them to clamber into one of the wagons and this they did, pulling the tarpaulin over their heads as the little Chinese girl told them that friends of hers would come to help them.

The four men lay there, sweating under the heavy covering, not knowing what to expect, until an hour later, they heard voices near the wagon. To McCormac's horror, he recognised one of the voices as Japanese. For one horrible moment they thought they were trapped. Then several people scrambled on to the tarpaulin and the train moved off. McCormac could hear voices chattering above them but no longer could he detect Japanese.

At last after about half an hour, the tarpaulin was lifted to reveal several Javanese. One of them beamed and told them they could come out now. They scrambled into the bright, blinding sunlight. They were among friends, the Javanese told them. The journey was to be a long one so he advised them to rest. In spite of McCormac's questions, the Javanese were reluctant to part with much information save for the fact that they had to reach Oosthaven.

Confident of their safety, the four men slept on top of the tarpaulin until dusk came and the Javanese woke them up. Now was their time to leave. The train slowed as it went up an incline and the four men dropped off into the long grass by the track side. Their fall from the train had been cushioned by the long grass and when they had all dropped out they scrambled away from the track and bolted into the jungle, trying to put as much distance as possible between them and the railway. Panting and exhausted they reached a clearing where they settled down for the night. The following day they set off once more, making reasonable headway. All, except Roy whose dysentery had returned, felt better and the going grew easier as they emerged from the jungle into wide expanses of grass. They continued like that for several days until they reached a village. More confident now, they walked straight in and were greeted by the head man who offered them his hospitality.

It was in this village that Skinny struck up a friendship with a nubile young native girl who followed him everywhere he went, tending him and granting him his every wish. It appeared that to have the affections of a white man was considered a prize beyond all prizes and Skinny took full advantage of it.

The village they had reached was only a few miles from their destination, Oosthaven, but they were warned by the head man that it was teeming with Japanese who often paid his village a visit. McCormac, nevertheless, felt confident of their security there, since the head man wore the coveted Queen Wilhelmina's Medal.

By then, though, Roy's dysentery had grown very much worse and now he contracted malaria. He vomited almost continually and it seemed that death was not far off for him. The natives of the village did what they could, trying all their own remedies but none of them seemed to work.

The village head man explained to McCormac that he and his people were poor and could offer little by way of food. He would, however, do all he could and he assured them of their safety in his village. He explained that the young men of his village worked as labourers for the Japanese and earned just enough money for their very basic needs. It transpired that the Japanese were not averse to employing Eurasians and on hearing this an idea occurred to McCormac. He could pass as a Eurasian but for his blue eyes. Determined somehow or other to repay the old man for his kindness, McCormac volunteered to go with the other young men of the village and find work with the Japanese, then he would be able to pay the old man with the money he earned.

The others could not believe their ears when they heard McCormac's suggestion. They thought he'd been affected by the sun. But McCormac was adamant and the following day he went with the other natives to Oosthaven. As he queued up to register with the other natives and caught sight of the Japanese soldier who was taking their names, he began to have second thoughts about the wisdom of his venture. But he realised it was too late to turn back then and soon his time came to confront the Jap. Inwardly he was trembling as the Jap eyed him suspiciously, immediately noting his blue eyes.

McCormac explained to the Jap that he had come from the north and was in search of work on his way to look for his parents who were living in the south. He was Eurasian, he explained, but the Jap questioned him about his blue eyes and McCormac replied without hesitation that his father was German. This seemed to satisfy the Jap and McCormac was put to work.

Every day, McCormac returned to his labours. The work was back-breaking, carrying dirt and wielding a huge hammer to break boulders. The hours were long and the work exhausting but true to his promise, he kept it up, giving the head man his pay at the end of each day.

But while McCormac laboured on, Roy was getting steadily worse and one evening he lapsed into a coma. He died that night and the following day McCormac, Donaldson and Skinny buried him. It was after the burial that the head man suggested it was time McCormac and the others were moving on. Their stay had been long enough and the longer they stayed the greater was the likelihood that the Japanese might tumble to the ruse and wipe out the entire village for helping them.

McCormac asked the old man if he could arrange a boat to take them across the narrow stretch of water that separates Sumatra and Java. The answer that came almost stunned McCormac. The man agreed to arrange it—providing Skinny married his daughter! It appeared that the relationship between Skinny and his daughter, Li Tong, had blossomed into romance but when McCormac explained to Skinny he was even more dumbfounded that Skinny agreed. He had fallen for the girl and pointed out that, like McCormac, he could pass as a Eurasian if any questions were asked by the Japs. Try as he might McCormac could not dissuade Skinny from staying. His mind had been made up.

That night McCormac and Donaldson boarded a fishing boat for the crossing and bade Skinny farewell. Both men watched the young British soldier standing by the water's edge with his bride-to-be waving until he was lost in the darkness. They could hardly believe that it had happened and McCormac and Donaldson sat in the boat with their own thoughts as it made its way across the stretch of water.

Their one fear was for Japanese launches which regularly patrolled the straits but they saw nothing of them and at last they put into an inlet on a small island. The fisherman at the helm told them to get off on to the beach while he went to check on some buoys. They did so and were left alone. It was then that it occurred to them that the fisherman had possibly taken fright and dumped them off to leave them to their own devices. They waited for some time before they heard the sound of the boat returning once more.

It must have been almost two hours before dawn when the boat crept into a tree-lined beach and they jumped off on to the sand. With the boat securely beached, the fisherman told them to wait where they were then he made off into the jungle.

The time dragged by as they waited for his return but finally he appeared almost an hour later with another man who beckoned them to follow. They thanked the fisherman then followed their new guide, a small Javanese with a sour face. They were in Java at last.

After what seemed like a marathon trek through the dense jungle, the Javanese stopped in his tracks when they reached a clearing. He turned to McCormac and told him that they would find friendly troops if they continued up the trail for just another two more miles. With that he left them alone in the jungle.

With no alternative but to believe the man, they struck out up the track but the going became increasingly difficult and after they had gone only a mile, they stopped to rest and gather some food. Both men lay by the edge of the track for some time, possibly hours, before suddenly they heard the sound of someone approaching. Before they could scramble for cover, a young man appeared round a bend in the track and stopped dead, gaping at them.

For a moment neither party spoke until Donaldson, taking the initiative, said:

'Who the hell are you?'

The newcomer didn't answer but threw the question back at them. Both escapers eyed him suspiciously. He was obviously not a native and spoke with a hint of an Australian accent. Most important, he was not Japanese and McCormac and Donaldson decided to come clean and they told him their story. He listened intently taking in all they said then admitted that he had known they were in Java. McCormac asked how he had found out but the stranger brushed aside the question and launched into an interrogation of them.

Both escapers were impressed by the man's wealth of information about them and quickly realised that he was no ordinary stray soldier lost in the jungle. But try as they might, they were unable to get the slightest inkling of who he was or where he had come from. Their mystery man was giving away no secrets.

The stranger led them farther up the track until they reached a small encampment consisting of a group of tents. They were led to one from which a fearsome man, dressed in a jungle green combat uniform and armed with a revolver, emerged. The 'Australian' introduced the man as the leader of a band of guerrillas operating in the area. They both thought he certainly looked the part with a nasty scar which ran down the length of his left cheek.

The guerrilla chief, Mansfelt by name, ordered Donaldson into his tent and told McCormac to wait. Inside he grilled Donaldson for some time, questioning every detail in his story until he was satisfied that he was genuine, then McCormac was subjected to the same treatment. At last he indicated that they could both stay and with that the Australian wished the two men 'good luck' and went off back down the trail. They never saw him again.

Mansfelt was as forthcoming with answers to their

questions as the other had been. He revealed nothing and advised both Donaldson and McCormac not to expect answers.

'The less you know, the less you can tell if you are captured by the Japs,' he warned them and they accepted his judgement.

McCormac and Donaldson stayed with the band of guerrillas for some time, often having to wait for days on end alone in the encampment, while the guerrillas went off to carry out raids on Japanese outposts. After each of these sorties, the ragged band of men would return with supplies of ammunition and rifles captured from the Japs. On every occasion Mansfelt told them how their score of dead Japs was mounting.

As the days passed, McCormac and Donaldson became impatient, itching for something to happen. They grew tired of waiting and were anxious to be on their way. McCormac badgered Mansfelt for some indication as to when they could move on, and every time they were assured it would be soon.

To break the almost unbearable monotony, McCormac asked Mansfelt if they could go on a raid with his band and, to his surprise, he agreed to take them along. They went deep into the jungle until Mansfelt told them to wait in hiding. They were left alone while the guerrillas went off. Soon they heard the sound of shots being fired not far off then suddenly there was silence. The minutes dragged by then the guerrillas returned, all of them grinning with pleasure. They had wiped out an entire Jap patrol and taken all their rifles and ammunition. With that they returned to the camp.

The days dragged on until one morning at dawn Mansfelt entered their tent with a Javanese native. It was time to move. Mansfelt wished them luck and they left, following the native along another track. For days they followed the little man who rarely spoke a word until at last they reached a village near the sea. The two men were left in the care of the head man who told them that they would be taken from there in due course—but to where and when, he refused to disclose. Another long wait, they thought, but they were wrong. Things began to move fast, for the first time. That night they were shepherded down to the beach where they boarded a junk with several Javanese on board.

The junk made off out to sea and they sailed all night until at dawn they found themselves off a coastline, but which one the Javanese would not tell them. They were put ashore and they rested all day until at night the junk put to sea once more. When the first light of day came, they again found themselves approaching another coastline with a village at its edge. But as the junk nosed in towards the shore there was an excited cry from one of the crew. He had spotted Japs in the village and the junk beat a hasty retreat.

For six days and nights the junk repeated the operation, calling in at villages during the day then sailing by night. On the sixth day the junk dropped anchor and Donaldson and McCormac jumped ashore as usual. They were taken to the village where they were confronted by a small, hairy man clad only in shorts and wearing an Aussie hat. He greeted them, then like the others beforehand, launched into a barrage of questions evading any the two escapers tried to ask. At last satisfied that the two men were in fact who they claimed to be he made a statement which left both of them staring at him open-mouthed.

'I'll radio Darwin and we'll get you out of here as soon as possible,' he said in an almost matter-of-fact way.

The two men couldn't believe their ears. This ragged little man was offering them a ticket home. When they had recovered from the initial shock, the two men bombarded him with questions but he resolutely refused to give them any answers and merely told them to get some rest in a nearby hut.

Still numbed and bewildered by what had happened, the two men waited for two days until on the evening of the second day, the Australian took them to the beach where he bade them farewell and helped them on board a junk. A little Javanese steered the boat well out to sea then when they were some distance from land, dropped anchor. Neither Donaldson nor McCormac could understand what was happening. They just waited there for what seemed like hours until McCormac heard the unmistakable sound of distant aircraft engines.

The little Javanese was tensed now, sitting up in the boat, clutching a powerful torch in his hand. They all strained their eyes for a glimpse of the aircraft then one of them saw it, a shadow in the night sky. Just then a lamp flashed on in the plane and the little Javanese flashed back in reply. Minutes later they saw the black shape of the flying-boat as it slid across the water.

The Javanese continued flashing at the plane as it homed in on the light. Minutes later they were being hauled aboard the aircraft and with a deafening roar the engines burst into life and they were soaring up into the night sky, still unable to believe what had happened. Twelve hours later the Catalina flying-boat landed at Darwin, Australia. They had made it.

Their journey from the hell of Panjang prison to Darwin had taken them five months and they had travelled over one thousand miles but although their staggering feat amazed all Australia, McCormac's mind was filled with more important things. More than anything else he desperately wanted to find out what had become of his wife. Time and again he asked but to his frustration no one seemed to be able to confirm or deny what Teruchi had claimed was the fate of the *Wakefield*. The thought of Pat's fate had plagued him all these months but it seemed no one could help him. Then the answer came quite by chance when one day he picked up a copy of the *Daily Mail* and there was a photograph of Pat with their newly born daughter. Teruchi, true to form, had been lying.

Charles McCormac was awarded the Distinguished Conduct Medal and commissioned, and by the end of the war he had attained the rank of squadron leader. The R.A.F. put his experiences in the jungle to good use and he was given the job of teaching young airmen the art of survival in the jungle. No man could have been more eminently qualified for such a task.

When Japan surrendered in 1945, McCormac was in Singapore and he attended the War Crimes Court. When the first accused was ushered into the dock, McCormac recognised him immediately as the vile creature who had interrogated him years earlier. It was Teruchi. McCormac had the satisfaction of watching him sentenced to death for the atrocities he had committed. The wheel of fortune had turned full circle.

# 5

# *Arctic Chase*

There are few countries in the world which can match Norway for the sheer, rugged majesty of its coastline. It stretches for hundreds of miles, penetrating deep into the heart of the Arctic Circle, with much of it held in the grip of the fierce Arctic winter for most of the year. During its short summer months the coastline with its awesome, mountainous fjords cutting deep into the mainland and the clusters of islands at their mouths, is a tourist attraction. In luxury cruise-ships thousands of sightseers sail into the fjords, some of which are as much as fifty miles long.

From the placid waters of the fjords, mountains covered permanently in a mantle of snow, soar skywards for thousands of feet. Around the base of these towering peaks lie tiny clusters of houses, remote outposts with few links with the outside world, from which the hardy Norsemen go to sea to make a meagre living as fishermen. By nature the Norwegian fisherman is a tough, hardy being; he has to be to survive in the extreme conditions under which he lives. This characteristic toughness and resolution of mind was exemplified by many Norwegians in the years of German occupation from 1940 to 1945 during the Second World War.

When Norway fell to the might of the German forces in 1940, many Norwegians fled the country, not to escape the wrath of their new overlords and save their skins but to fight on from Britain in whatever way they could in a bid to rid their beloved country of the Nazi terror. These courageous men fought in the air, on land and at sea, many of them giving their lives that one day Norway should be free again.

Their land and particularly its coastline was vital to Hitler's war strategy. His merchant ships, carrying war materials such as fish-oil from the captured factories of north Norway, could sail almost the entire length of the country sheltered by the hundreds of islands along the coast. They could do so with almost complete impunity since British submarines could not operate successfully in the shallow waters between island and mainland and surface warships venturing there did so at their peril. They plied these waters at the mercy of strategically placed batteries of heavy guns which could pound them to destruction from their island emplacements. Furthermore the fjords offered the German navy an ideal anchorage for their giant battleships, like the *Bismarck*, *Gneisenau* and *Tirpitz*. From there, Hitler planned, they would operate against the British Fleet and merchantmen in the North Sea and North Atlantic, darting out to wreak havoc among the convoys then scurrying back into the sanctuary of the fjords to refuel and re-arm. In theory this plan of attack looked good but in practice it was not so perfect; but that is another story.

Perhaps the greatest advantage Hitler held in capturing Norway was its airfields. From these, the German Luftwaffe could operate against British shipping in the North Sea and against Britain itself, bombing the towns and cities of Scotland, northern England and the east coast. In addition, the Luftwaffe could keep an ever watchful eye open for intruders into Norwegian waters and fly cover for the German merchantmen making their way down the coast to Germany.

The existence of these heavily defended fighter and bomber bases down the length of Norway gave the British High Command grave cause for concern. Convoys taking supplies to Russia suffered badly at the hands of the Luftwaffe and thousands of tons of these crucial supplies were sent to the bottom of the sea. Aerial attack on the German bases in the far north of Norway was fraught with difficulties because of the limited range of British bombers, which on such missions had to fly without fighter cover because of the even shorter range of the Spitfire and Hurricane fighters. There was only one sure-fire way of hitting at these remote airfields and that was by sabotage; by sending groups of agents into the country armed with explosives to destroy the German aircraft and their fields from the ground.

The British quickly realised that it would be suicide to send anyone other than a Norwegian on such missions. Only the Norwegians who had been born and bred into the wilds of that country could survive its rigours. One such man was Jan Baalsrud, whose story this is ...

Baalsrud was one of those who chose to leave his country rather than live under the Nazi jackboot when the German army swept through his country. He lived in Oslo working as a watchmaker in his father's business and had only just finished his apprenticeship when the Germans launched their attack. He joined the ranks of the Norwegian army and took part in the bitter fighting until Norway was crushed into defeat. Determined not to take it lying down he escaped to neutral Sweden and there joined forces with a Norwegian organisation which had been set up in Stockholm to help his fellow countrymen escape from Norway. He volunteered for what was perhaps the most dangerous work of all, acting as a courier between Stockholm and Oslo returning to his country time and time again, risking capture and certain execution if he were caught. Such activities were, of course, contrary to the rules governing Sweden's neutrality and eventually he was arrested by the Swedish police and imprisoned for five months. Perhaps it is as well that he was caught by the Swedes for, had he been caught by the Germans while carrying out his clandestine forays into Norway, he would undoubtedly have suffered torture of the most horrible kind before being killed.

After having served only three months of his sentence, Baalsrud was released and given two weeks to get out of the country but even this presented him with a problem. Where was he to go? He was still in his early twenties, a short but robust man with dark hair and grey-blue eyes. He still had an excess of adventurous spirit which drove him on to seek new and exciting ways of fighting for his country. He determined to reach Britain but his ultimate travels were to take him on a most circuitous route. He succeeded in reaching Russia then on to Bulgaria, Egypt, Aden, Bombay, South Africa, America and Canada then on to England. During his travels he teamed up with another Norwegian, Per Blindheim, who had much the same aim in life as Jan. The two men were destined to share many adventures together. Quite by chance, not long after they had arrived in England, they met up with an English officer whom Jan had known in Stockholm. They talked at length and the two young men explained that they wanted to do something to hit back at the Germans. Without delay they were enlisted into the Linge Company, one of the most famous Norwegian units operating from Britain.

The Linge Company was a special commando unit comprised entirely of Norwegians recruited by Martin Linge, a courageous Norwegian who had escaped from Norway and come to Britain to carry on the fight. Linge's commandos went through all the rigours of commando training just as the British units did, training with them and carrying out raids on strategic targets in Norway, the most notable of which were the raids on the Lofoten Islands and Vaagso, during which Captain Linge was killed fighting at the head of his men. To be selected for service with such a company was a signal honour for the two young men and they launched themselves into their training with all the passion and enthusiasm they could muster.

Jan and Per were inseparable during these long months of training in the highlands of Scotland. To describe their training as 'tough' would be a gross understatement of the truth. Its object was to transform them into hard-bitten fighters who could survive under the worst conditions and carry out missions in almost impossible circumstances—alone if necessary. They were taught all the arts of clandestine warfare from unarmed combat to demolition work. They became expert in the use of explosives; with small arms they became crack marksmen. They were force-marched often for fifty or sixty miles carrying heavy packs, then at the end of it given a difficult target to attack and expected to fight their way to it in the process. They soon became superbly fit and capable of amazing feats of endurance. They could strip down their automatic weapons and those used by the Germans *blindfold*. They were not to know when they might have to use enemy arms but they had to be prepared for any and every eventuality. Both men emerged from their training in the peak of condition and ready to go to war. They wanted to get back to Norway and strike at the Germans on their home ground. Their chance was soon to come....

During the years of German occupation of Norway, there existed a highly secret 'passenger service' between the Shetland Islands, the closest British-held land, and Norway. Using small Norwegian fishing boats to carry them, weapons, agents and supplies were ferried across the wild expanse of sea between the islands and Norway. On their return journeys, the boats carried refugees whose lives were in danger by remaining in Norway. This special service soon became known as 'The Shetland Bus' and the adventures of the men who sailed these small craft are legion. (In his book *The Shetland Bus*, published by Nelson in 1951, David Howarth, who helped organise the voyages, tells of the heroism of these men.) Jan Baalsrud and his friend Per were to become passengers on one of the famous Shetland buses when they, along with four other special agents, were given the task of returning to their native Norway and wreaking havoc among the Germans.

The party of specially trained saboteurs was to be led by Sigurd Eskeland, a tough, hardened commando who, like the others, had answered the call to arms when his country was invaded. With him were to go Jan, Per and a radio operator called Salvesen who could work wonders with a wireless. Their brief for the mission was short and to the point. They were to cross the thousand miles of ocean from Shetland to north Norway, set up a base there and recruit and train local people as saboteurs. But most of all they had one job in particular which had to be carried out at all cost. They were to attack the German airfield at Bardufoss, wreck planes, demolish buildings and kill as many Germans as possible. Their orders were straightforward but the mission was fraught with some of the most unbelievable hazards, not the least of which was getting across the vast expanse of ocean undetected.

The group duly assembled at Scalloway in the Shetlands and preparations began for the mission in March 1943. A boat called the *Brattholm* was chosen for the voyage. A more unlikely craft for the trip it would have been difficult to find. She was around seventy-five feet long and powered by a single engine which gave her a speed of only eight knots. In appearance she looked like any of the other hundreds of Norwegian fishing boats which fished the coastal waters and this was what the planners of the raid hoped the Germans would think if she were sighted by a patrol boat or aircraft. Beneath this seemingly innocent exterior lay a sinister cargo and arsenal of weaponry. She was armed with no less than seven machine-guns in disguised mountings on deck and, in addition to this armament, each one of the passengers was allotted his own machine-gun which he kept hidden in case of emergencies. Furthermore, some eight tons of explosives were hidden in the hold along with weapons, a store of food, winter clothing and radio transmitters. In fact the little fishing vessel was rather like a floating powder keg. The explosives themselves were equipped with a series of fuses, each of a different time duration and one of which was instantaneous. The idea was that if they were attacked or discovered by the Germans and escape was impossible, they would blow up the boat—and probably themselves with it. On no account could they afford to let the cargo or secret information about anti-German agents in Norway fall into German hands.

For the little band of agents and the eight man crew of the boat, theirs was to be a maiden voyage in more ways than one. None of the boats which operated out of the Shetlands had ever undertaken the thousand-mile-long trip to the far north of Norway. All the other expeditions had been to the southern part of the country which was considerably nearer. The skipper was confident, however, that his boat could make the voyage. After all he had come from that part of Norway to the Shetlands and in addition there were fewer Germans in the far north to keep watch on the coast, but this was by no means an assurance that the voyage would go without event.

On the appointed day, the *Brattholm* slipped out of

the harbour to begin her epic voyage and was soon out to sea, braving the mountainous waves and violent storms that rage in that part of the ocean. Throughout the journey ever watchful eyes scanned the sea and air for the slightest hint of the enemy; for the warship that could blast them out of the sea with a single salvo or the aircraft that could swoop down on them and strafe them into oblivion or send fast patrol boats after them in a bid to capture them intact. As it turned out, luck was with them during the entire journey and it went without event. If indeed they had been spotted by the Germans then their ruse had worked and they had been accepted as being Norwegian fishermen. But the telling time had yet to come and was almost upon them when they edged into the Arctic coast, where German watchers were almost certain to see them from their vantage points amid the mountainous snow-covered hills on the islands.

The real test of their disguise came when they nosed in towards the island of Senja. As they did they sighted a trawler coursing through the sea towards them. On closer inspection they saw that it was armed. It was a German patrol boat and none had been reported in that area. They changed course away from it and luckily it did not follow. They had proved their disguise had worked. But their original landing point was obviously too dangerous so they headed farther north and decided to land in a bay on the island of Ribbenesöy some thirty miles away.

The boat ploughed through the waves until late that afternoon, then it turned inland, rounded the island of Ribbenesöy and nosed into Toftefjord. They had chosen their anchorage well since there was little or no habitation and they were screened from the sea by the island, and really only visible from the air. The fjord and the great snow-covered hills around it were desolate and an air of peace and tranquillity hung over the place. The water was a flat calm and little stirred. For the men on board the *Brattholm* it seemed as if they were in another world, far off from the hell of war but in a few short hours their silent haven was to become the graveyard for all but one of them.

For the moment all was peaceful as the anchor slipped into the calm waters and they took their first look round the surrounding hills. It was then that they saw the tiny cottage at the foot of a hill at the back of the bay, with a thin column of smoke creeping lazily from its chimney. It was clear that the cottage was occupied—but by whom? Most important of all, were they friendly? Not all Norwegians were loyal to their country. Some were Nazis and followers of the traitor Quisling who headed the pro-German puppet government which ruled the country with an iron fist, spreading fear among the population.

The Gestapo, with all its vile methods, held the country in the grip of fear and Norwegians soon came to learn not to trust a stranger. The Gestapo had devised a way of testing a man's loyalty to the new regime. They would 'plant' one of their men posing as an agent who had come from England and if the innocent Norwegian gave him help or succour, the Gestapo would swoop. If the bewildered Norwegian was not immediately executed he would certainly be sent off to a concentration camp in Germany to suffer a lingering horrible death. Worse still, his family would suffer. It was little wonder, therefore, that every stranger was treated with suspicion.

Eskeland and his companions knew of the Gestapo's methods and were aware of the difficulties they were bound to face amongst the population. Outwardly one could not tell friend from foe; the helpers from those who, through either fear or loyalty to the Quislings, would betray them to the Germans. They did, however, have the names of those whom they could certainly trust, those who had already committed themselves to the fight against the Germans. But in their search for those people they would inevitably have to deal with some whose loyalty to the king was in doubt.

They had no sooner arrived in the country than they were faced with just such a problem. Somehow they had to determine whether the folk who lived in that cottage were with them or against them. It fell to Eskeland and the skipper of the boat to find out. They rowed ashore and approached the cottage. Anything, they knew, could happen now and the men on the boat waited with apprehension for the outcome of Eskeland's knock on the cottage door. Luck was with them, however, for they found only an old woman with her grandchildren. During the conversation that he had with the old lady, Eskeland gave no hint of where they had come from or who they really were. He told her they were fishermen who had taken shelter in the fjord to do some engine repairs. Since this was not an uncommon occurrence, the old lady gave no indication of doubting their word.

It was with some considerable relief that they also learned there were no Germans in the country around the fjord—or so at least the woman thought. In any event, loyal or not, the ageing woman could do little to harm them since she had no telephone with which to raise an alarm even if she had wanted to. With that, the two men returned to the boat and all had a hearty meal, joyous at being back in their homeland. But however great their emotions were upon their return, they did not for a moment forget that danger could lurk in these hills and a constant watch was kept for anything remotely suspicious.

The skipper of the *Brattholm* was anxious to get under way again as soon as possible and that meant finding a landing place and hide for their precious cargo. Concealing eight tons of explosives, together with a batch of weapons and radio transmitters, was to be no mean feat and they would almost certainly need local help to find a suitable place. Once more they were posed with the problem of whom they should go to for help. On the list of names Eskeland had been given in England, there was that of a shopkeeper at Ribbenesöy. None of the men on the boat had ever met the man but London had said that he could be trusted, so Eskeland decided that he would pay him a visit.

As darkness came to the fjord, Eskeland and the ship's engineer along with another crewman set off in a small powered boat to visit the man. The boat cruised through the placid waters of the bay then round the coast of the island until it came to a point opposite a tiny cluster of buildings, one of which was the shop they were looking for. The windows of the shop glowed with light. At least someone was at home. By the shore in front of the shop was a small fishing boat with three men on board. In a tiny outpost where everyone knew everyone else, it was quite an event for strangers to arrive so they would have to explain away their presence. Eskeland pulled alongside the fishing boat and hailed the three men. He explained that their fishing boat had suffered engine trouble and they were anxious to get to Tromso to pick up spare parts. The upshot of the conversation was that one of the fishermen told them that the shopkeeper had a small boat in which he might be willing to take them to Tromso. With that, Eskeland thanked them and jumped on to the shore.

He made his way up to the shop and knocked on the door. For the first time since they had reached Norway he would soon have to reveal the true identity and purpose of their mission but he had to be wary. After a few moments, the shopkeeper opened the door. He had been in bed and was in his night clothes. At first, Eskeland merely told him that they were fishermen, trying to put the man at ease and size him up at the same time. At last he told the man bluntly that they had come from England and instantly the man's face went ashen white. He had agreed to take them to Tromso but now his attitude changed dramatically. He was nervous and trembling. He made excuses saying that he couldn't help them. The risks were too great. He had his wife and family to think of.

At this Eskeland and the others became puzzled at his reluctance to help them. He had been recommended to them in England. And then the horrible truth was revealed to them. He was not the man they had been looking for. He explained that the previous owner of the shop had died not long before and he had taken over the shop. Furthermore they both had *the same name*. Of all the mistakes to make, this was the worst. What could they do with the man? Could they rely on him to keep his mouth shut or would he go running to the Germans? It must be remembered that the man in all probability thought that they were Gestapo agents setting a trap for him. If he didn't report them then that would mark him as a traitor to the new regime. What were they to do? They couldn't kill the man to keep him quiet. That would have devastating consequences. At last they made him promise not to reveal their presence to the Germans and this he did. He even suggested the names of two other men who might be willing to help them and with that Eskeland and the others left and got under way in the dinghy once more.

They got back to the *Brattholm* and told the others what had happened. This they all agreed added a new urgency to their need to act fast and Eskeland set off to find the two fishermen the shopkeeper had recommended. At last he found them and they willingly agreed to help. At least the shopkeeper had not sent them into a trap. The two men said they would come to the *Brattholm* the following afternoon and help them unload the cargo and stow it in some deserted caves they knew would make an ideal hide. Grateful for the offer of help, Eskeland thanked them and left but it was almost dawn before he returned to the fishing boat. By then he had been betrayed to the Germans.

The shopkeeper, however reluctantly he did it, had tipped off a Nazi sympathiser of their presence and already the Germans were planning their attack.*

The morning passed quietly without sight or sound of anyone in the bay. This gave Eskeland and the others cause to believe that the shopkeeper had been true to his word and had not betrayed them. They reasoned that had he done so, something would certainly have happened but how wrong they were . . .

Just before mid-day, Eskeland and his party went below deck to get some sleep while the crew of the *Brattholm* kept watch. Then a little after noon, the alarm was raised —a German warship swept into the bay. Eskeland and the others tumbled out of their bunks and dashed to the deck but just as they did so, the warship's guns thundered. The tranquillity of the fjord was shattered in one swift blow and shells exploded in the water around the *Brattholm*, heaving great plumes of water into the air. There was no way of escape and each man knew exactly what had to be done. Eskeland ordered the ship to be abandoned while one of the men raised the naval flag to the mast.

The crew of the *Brattholm* lowered a boat and rowed with all their might for the shore while Eskeland and Per scrambled into the hold to light the five-minute fuse on the eight tons of explosives. Meanwhile Jan and Salvesen poured petrol over the cipher books and set light to them. Then they lowered the other dinghy on the lee of the ship to wait for the other two to finish their work.

Meanwhile the German warship had stopped and two

* After the war, a Norwegian court sentenced the shopkeeper to eight years hard labour for betraying the patriots.

small boats crammed with troops pulled away from it to land on shore. Then the warship got under way again with her guns blazing. Eskeland and Per dropped into the dinghy and there the four men waited keeping the fishing boat between them and the warship until the last moment before pulling away.

By then the warship was closing in and Jan grabbed a machine-gun and emptied a whole magazine at the bridge of the warship, raking it with fire. Then he ducked down once more, protected by the *Brattholm*. From where they were the men in the dinghy could see the *Brattholm*'s crew had reached the shore but already they had suffered casualties. They were swamped by German troops who fired on the defenceless men, killing some and capturing the others. The whole of the bay resounded to the chatter of machine-gun fire and the boom of the warship's heavy gun.

Now was the time to move and as the seconds ticked by and the fuse on the eight tons of explosives burned away, Eskeland and the others rowed like mad away from the fishing boat. They had almost two hundred yards to go before reaching the shore and they rowed like demons as the German machine-guns opened up on them, riddling the boat with bullets. Gradually she began to sink but miraculously none of the occupants had been injured. Just then the warship drew alongside the *Brattholm* and at that precise moment the fishing boat was rocked by an explosion but only the primer had exploded. For a horrible moment the men in the dinghy thought the rest of the explosives would not ignite and the Germans would capture the *Brattholm*. That would be disastrous.

They continued to row while the German heavy guns sent shells plunging into the water around them. Then seconds later there was an almighty, thundering roar as the eight tons of explosives blew up. *Brattholm* disappeared for ever in one stroke and debris was showered over a vast area. The force of the blast tossed Eskeland into the water but Jan pulled him back into the boat. As the noise of the explosion died away the German heavy gun came into play again and a well aimed shell streaked towards the dinghy with a high-pitched whine and blew the dinghy to bits, throwing the occupants into the water.

By some miracle none of them had been killed and they struck out for the shore but then the German machine-guns opened up on them lashing the water with fire. They all succeeded in reaching the shore but as they did so and scrambled to their feet, the Germans were presented with easier targets. Per took a bullet in the head and fell dead to the ground while Salvesen too was hit. Jan Baalsrud scrambled on and dived behind a boulder where he found cover from the bullets which thudded into the ground around him. The Germans were swarming towards him. He was alone and they were closing in fast. Then he spotted a small mound not far off which was covered with young trees and afforded better cover. He leapt to his feet and charged towards it, limping as he went because he had lost one of his sea-boots during the swim for shore.

It seemed as if all hell had been let loose as bullets whipped into the snow around him. He darted through the trees and ran almost headlong into one of the German patrols. He scurried away from them as they drew a bead on him and in desperation he clawed his way up a steep slope, trying to scale the high hill at the back of the bay, but the troops were closing in on him fast. The officer at their head drew his pistol and fired but his bullet missed Jan by only inches. He continued to scramble up the hill battling against the snow which caused him to slip as he climbed higher. The officer yelled at him to stop but Jan charged blindly on, then as the German closed on him Baalsrud halted, turned and levelled his pistol at the officer. He squeezed the trigger—but nothing happened. The mechanism was frozen solid. He pulled the trigger again and again but it refused to fire then he ejected two bullets and fired. This time it worked and smacked a bullet into the German officer. He sagged at the knees and Jan fired again, killing him. The body reeled backwards and rolled down the slope to where the Germans had stopped in their tracks.

Jan scrambled on up the slope as bullets lashed the snow around him. One caught his bare right foot and severed half of his big toe but he charged on. The warship's heavy gun opened up and shells pounded into the snow casting it into the sky to rain down on Jan. At last, fighting for breath, he reached the top of the hill and scrambled into cover.

From his vantage point he could survey the scene in the fjord. It was one of chaos with German troops rounding up the crew and dragging off the bodies of his dead comrades. A desolate feeling of loneliness swept over Jan but the powerful urge to survive overcame it. His situation seemed hopeless but he was not going to submit without a fight. Somehow he had to escape the Germans who were sweeping up the hill towards him or die in the attempt. He hobbled out of cover, away from the bay, to begin one of the epic bids for freedom in the annals of escape history.

Jan had no idea then whether or not any of the others had managed to escape and it was not until much later that he eventually discovered what had become of them. Those who were not killed in the fight were executed by the Gestapo. Jan Baalsrud was the sole survivor. But how long could he survive? His situation was perilous in the extreme. He was on a tiny island, wounded in one foot, soaked through to the skin and in danger of freezing to death. Without help and shelter soon he would either die at the hands of the Germans or slowly succumb to the cold. His only hope of evading capture was to reach the mainland. Soon the island would be swarming with Germans bent on tracking him down.

But in the meantime his only thought was to put as much ground as possible between him and the pursuing Germans. He struggled on over the hills, fighting off the pain he felt in his right foot until at last he reached the far side of the island. There was less snow there and he took advantage of some of the bare patches to lay a false trail. He scrambled on from there down to the shore and the narrow stretch of beach which skirted it. Somehow he had to get off the island for, sooner or later, the Germans would find him if he did not. He half ran along the beach which was free of snow and therefore left no tracks to follow. Then he came to a narrow sound in which were vast rocks protruding out of the water. Baalsrud stopped. The nearest of the huge rocks was about fifty yards away and to the desperate man that meant sanctuary. Without hesitation he charged into the water and began to swim across to the rocks, pushing aside great chunks of ice as he swam. At last, breathless and aching from head to foot, he pulled himself up on to the great mound.

Casting a glance behind him he could see the Germans scouring the island he had just left but it had not occurred to them to cast a glance over the water. Jan pulled himself up the rocky beach until he found a patch of peat-covered ground. Some of the peat had been cut away to form a sort of ditch and he crawled into this and began to do exercises to keep his body warm. While he did so, he watched the Germans scurrying about the island in search of him. Soon, the Arctic night began to fall and he saw the search continue by torch-light.

His exercises were slowly bringing the circulation back to his body but with it came a terrible pain from his foot. His clothes were soaked and he knew for certain that if he stayed there all night he would die—above all else, he had to keep on the move. In fact he had to get off his rocky haven. Pulling himself up he tried to survey the area, looking for a way out. Return to the island from which he had come was out of the question but there was one faint ray of hope left. There was yet another island about 250 yards from his rock with a single house on it. If he could reach there perhaps he might find shelter on it. Without the warmth of a fire he would be doomed to freeze to death.

For the second time, he plunged into the freezing water and began to swim. The strain of the swim was agonising and he would never have made it had it not been for the strong current which helped him on his way. With the last vestige of energy drawn from him, his body was swept up on to the shore. He could manage to crawl only a few feet before utter fatigue finally overtook him and he lapsed into unconsciousness. Jan Baalsrud might well have died where he lay had it not been for fate taking a hand. Luck plays the biggest part in the success of the escaper and it was with Jan Baalsrud.

The following morning, two children came down to the beach to play among the rocks and there they found the unconscious man. It was then that he slowly began to come to and through the haze of pain and half-consciousness, he saw the two small children. In spite of his condition he could see that they were both terrified and on the point of running away in fright. At all cost, Jan had to allay their fears. He talked to them as gently as he could, explaining that there was no need to be afraid. He had had an accident and needed help. Gradually they relaxed. Hauling himself to his feet, he asked if they would take him to their home and they led him off to a small house nearby.

Jan had no idea of the sort of reception he might get but his situation was so desperate that he had to take a chance. When he arrived at the house, he found two women with some more children. Both women had husbands but they were away fishing and were not likely to return for some time. Jan could not have been more fortunate. He had landed among friends and was given food from their meagre rations and warmth by a roaring fire. His wound was bandaged and life began to return to his frozen body. The women fussed over him like mothers over a child, careless of the fact that in doing so they were risking their lives.

Shortly after Jan's arrival at the house, the eldest son of one of the women arrived and was told Jan's story. Together they discussed where he would go from there. Jan's ultimate aim was obvious. He had to get out of Norway, and quickly. There were really only two alternatives open to him. One was to make contact with the Underground Movement and return to Britain via the Shetland Bus, but this might mean having to travel to the south of Norway for the pick up and result in his being exposed to capture all the way. The other alternative was to make for Sweden which was only eighty miles away from where he was. This, however, meant a journey over some of the most inhospitable and difficult country in the world.

They weighed up the prospects of his success by both routes and finally decided upon trying for Sweden. There was less chance of encountering Germans that way but the hazards he was likely to face making his way over the towering snow-covered and storm-bound mountains presented a formidable obstacle. Jan, however, was a man who knew the ways of the mountains. He was an expert skier, a first class mountaineer and had been trained to the peak of efficiency in the art of survival in the snowy wastes of the Arctic. But as things stood at that time, he was in effect imprisoned on the island. If the Germans came, there would be no chance of escape from the island. He had to get off it soon.

The boy told him that he had a rowing boat which he

could use to take him to the island of Ringvassöy where he knew a man who could ferry him to the mainland. The following day as the first light of dawn was spreading over the island, Jan and the boy made off in the rowing boat for the island of Ringvassöy. All was quiet and peaceful on the short voyage and at last they reached the island where Jan insisted the boy let him off the boat out of sight of the cluster of houses where he was to meet the man who would take him to the mainland.

It was still dark when he made his way to the house which the boy had told him belonged to a man called Jensen who would help him. Once there he knocked on the door and it was answered by a woman.

Jan enquired whether or not Jensen was in and was told that he was not and would not be there for some time. This left Jan in a difficult position. Who could he turn to now for help? He decided to take a chance and admitted to the woman that he was on the run from the Germans. The woman, it transpired, was Jensen's wife and the local midwife. Luck was with Jan again for the woman volunteered to give him shelter. He entered the house and was given food which he ate ravenously but already he had decided that it was too dangerous to wait in the house. He had hoped to leave immediately upon arrival but now that there was a delay, that put a different complexion on things. He decided to move on and make his way to the south of the island.

The midwife had told him that almost all the island folk could be trusted and that he would have no difficulty in finding a boat. With that he stepped out of the house and into the light of day. He made his way through the cluster of houses and up into the hills then struck out for the south of the island. For the next four days, he made his way around the coast and over the hills, making the journey in long bursts of walking sometimes twenty-four hours at a stretch. The going was difficult. There were no roads and few tracks so it was a trek over virgin territory all the way. Often he had to back-track after coming to an impassable cliff or great drifts of snow.

During the thirty-mile trek, he met only a few people but they were friendly and offered help willingly even to the extent of allowing him to spend the night in their houses. He made a point of asking his hosts if they knew of anyone who could ferry him across to the mainland and from each of them he got the same reply, Einer Sörensen. Above all others he was a man to be trusted. He operated the island's telephone exchange and lived in Bjorneskar, a small hamlet on the south of the island. There was, however, a problem in getting to him. That part of the island was crawling with Germans but Jan realised that if he were to get to the mainland at all, he would have to contact Sörensen.

Throughout his trek Jan suffered almost unbearable pain from his injured toe but at last, on the fourth day, he reached the high land overlooking Bjorneskar. He could see it clearly and across the sound, the mainland of Norway. When night came he made his way to Sörensen's house and as he expected was made welcome. He told the man only those parts of his story he dared reveal and Einer instantly offered to help in any way he could, agreeing to take him across to the mainland.

Einer decided that the best time to move would be that night. There was a storm brewing so he knew that there would be no German patrol boats out but he would need another pair of strong arms to row the distance so he roused his father, Bernhard Sörensen, from his sleep and told him of his plan. Like his son, Bernhard Sörensen was a man of unquestionable loyalty and he got himself ready for the journey. This remarkable man thought nothing of the prospect of undertaking the ten-mile row across to the mainland even at the age of seventy-two.

At dead of night while the storm was growing in intensity, they clambered into the small rowing boat to begin their journey. Weak from exhaustion, Jan could offer no help with the rowing. He made one attempt but his arms felt like jelly so the two others bent their backs and heaved on the huge oars, coursing the boat through the waves. Navigation across the stretch of water was made difficult by a heavy fall of snow and the mainland was obscured in the darkness. However by some sixth sense the Sörensens guided the boat across the wide stretch of water, disregarding the German searchlights which continually swept the dark sea.

At last, at around three o'clock in the morning, the boat bumped into the shore and Jan set foot on the mainland. Before parting, the Sörensens told him of a man who would help. His name was Lockertsen and he lived in a house in Snarby, close by where they had landed. He could, they said, be trusted to help.

Jan's most significant acquisition was a pair of skis which Einer Sörensen had given him. These above all would give him the edge over the Germans. He was an expert skier and could travel remarkable distances over snow-covered ground in a day, sometimes as much as fifty miles.

With his skis slung over his shoulder, he thanked the two Sörensens for their help and made off towards Lockertsen's house. He approached it cautiously in the dark then slipped round to the door. He gave it a push and to his amazement, it opened. All was dark inside and he entered but moments later a veritable mountain of a man came thundering down the stairs. This was Lockertsen and he had the look of a killer in his eyes as he saw the intruder.

Jan quickly explained that he was on the run from the Germans and that he had made his way across the sound with the help of some friends. He explained to Lockertsen that for the sake of his friends' safety he could not reveal their names. Jan's whole story sounded like a piece of fantasy to Lockertsen. It smelled of something sinister; like a trap. The story was not helped by the fact that Jan was on the point of exhaustion, not having slept for two days. In fact he could hardly talk coherently.

Baalsrud dared not reveal any more than he had, since the first rule of the agent was to tell as little as possible so that if his helper were taken by the Germans and questioned under torture, he would not be able to give away the names of others. In fact not once had he revealed his true identity to the many people who had given him a helping hand. He was dressed in the uniform of a Norwegian sailor and he kept up the pretence that he was just what he appeared to be. In all the story sounded utterly implausible to Lockertsen who made Jan repeat it no less than three times. The man was now in a position similar to the one experienced by the shopkeeper.

At last, however, Jan could keep his eyes open no longer and fell into a deep sleep, lying motionless on the floor. Lockertsen was a brave and courageous man who would risk all for his country but he was troubled by the thought that Jan might be a 'plant' or even a German deserter. If he were either of these and Lockertsen helped him, he would be in real trouble. As it was, though, the man was obviously exhausted and Lockertsen decided that the best course was to let him sleep. But Lockertsen didn't get any sleep that night. He stayed in the room watching the man and pondering on what he should do with him.

Just before dawn Lockertsen bent over the prostrate man and gave him a shake to wake him. With the instinctive reaction of a hunted man, Jan was awake instantly and leapt to his feet, drawing his pistol as he did so, imagining in his subconscious that he had been discovered by the Germans and intent on fighting his way out. Without realising what he was doing he waved the muzzle in Lockertsen's face and was on the point of pulling the trigger. This, Lockertsen decided, was no German. As Jan shook himself from his sleep, he realised what he had done. Certain now that the man who had come uninvited into his home was a fugitive, he ushered him into his loft where he said he could finish his sleep.

It was mid-day before Jan awoke once more and now that he was refreshed after his rest he was better able to explain himself to Lockertsen who offered all the help he could give. Jan told him that he was making for Sweden and that he intended heading over the mountains. He could have merely headed south and eventually come to Sweden but by that route he would be venturing near Tromso, which was the biggest German base in north Norway.

To cross the mountains was a hazardous undertaking by any standards. Although the Swedish border was not far off as the crow flies, he was faced with scaling vast mountains, some of them thousands of feet high, or trudging through valleys deep with snow. The country between him and the border was amongst the most treacherous in all Norway with every conceivable kind of danger ranging from terrifying storms, which could be whipped up in an instant, to the equally dangerous mists which could envelop a climber in seconds, leaving him lost to wander into untold dangers. The mountains were often precipitous, with cliffs dropping sheer for hundreds of feet. In poor visibility this could mean death for a climber.

There was, however, one consolation which Lockertsen pointed out. He had a motor boat in which he said he could take Jan at least twenty miles of the way. Ullsfjord, one of Norway's longest, cut deep into the mountains through which Jan would have to pass and Lockertsen offered to take him part of the way up the fjord, thus cutting out a great deal of climbing for Jan.

Lockertsen explained that there was a winter and summer track at the point where he would drop him off and he could follow one of these until he reached yet another fjord, the one which skirted the high plateau across which he would have to travel to reach the border. This was more than Jan could have hoped for. It would give him a good start over the mountains. Lockertsen recruited a friend and they set off in a boat loaded with fishing gear. Should they be stopped by the Germans they would claim to be fishing.

They travelled through the night down the dark waters of the fjord with the towering peaks rising almost sheer from the water's edge until they reached a jetty at the mouth of a smaller fjord. There, Jan disembarked and with heartfelt thanks bade them farewell. He donned his skis and made off down a rough snow-covered road which ran alongside the fjord. For the first time he moved with speed, his skis sliding over the crisp snow but his haste had to be tempered with caution for there were villages on that road through which he would have to pass or skirt around.

He had travelled some distance when he finally saw a check point ahead of him, barring his way along the road, but he veered off the track and succeeded in by-passing it. Then he returned to the road once more and hurtled along it. It was now getting light and the danger of being spotted was ever present but speed was of the essence and he prepared to take the chance. He shot along the road with his skis carving twin tracks in the snow until he came to a bend in the road. Before rounding the bend he could see the tops of some houses. He'd reached the first village. Then his heart almost stopped beating for when he swept round the bend, there ahead of him was a crowd of Germans on the road and they were being joined by others. But there was no stopping now.

Boldly he swept on down the road towards the Germans who milled over it. His heart thumped faster as he drew closer to them but then, as he plunged towards them, they parted and allowed him to sweep through without as much as a second glance. His bold attempt had paid off and the Germans hadn't even noticed the Norwegian naval uniform he was wearing but as he dashed on farther down the road, he felt that every German eye was on him and he waited with sickening suspense for the crack of a rifle. But it did not come.

Jan charged on through the village, weaving between the houses until there, dead ahead of him, was another group of German soldiers but this time he had run almost straight into a check point. The road block was only fifty yards away. He dared not go to it so he skidded off to the right on his skis, through a gate and began to make his way up the hillside ... too late. He'd been spotted. There were cries to halt but Jan charged on. Then came the bullets whining past his head and thudding into the snow around him.

He darted into some trees and continued to climb, watching a posse of soldiers trying vainly to scramble up the hill after him but for the first time he had the advantage of them. His mastery of the skis gave him the speed which his pursuers lacked. He passed through the wooded part of the steep hill and on to the bare white snow. From the base of the hill he looked like a small black ant fighting its way across the blanket of snow.

Jan could see the outline of the road far below him and he struck out across the face of the hills running parallel to the road. As long as he kept the fjord in sight, he knew he would be on the right track. By then he had left his hunters far behind and they hadn't a hope of catching him but the fact that he had been spotted worried him. Now the Germans would know where he was and the hunt for him would be intensified in that area.

When he had put a great enough distance between himself and his pursuers, he stopped for a rest and for the first time was able to drink in the spectacular beauty of his surroundings. From his vantage point he could see the wide plateau across Lyngenfjord. Over the plateau lay his goal—the frontier. But between him and that frontier, although not very far off, lay wild country in which he was to suffer the worst of the agonies of his marathon trek...

He did not linger long but started off again and by mid-day had covered the staggering distance of twenty miles but then he saw the first hints of danger sweeping over the towering peaks high above him—the first telltale signs of a storm brewing. Dark clouds gathered over the mountains and a strong wind whipped the fresh snow off their peaks. The clouds brought snow enveloping him in a swirling white mass. Almost instantly his visibility was cut to only a few yards. He was perched on the edge of a mountain, almost three thousand feet from its base, with dangers waiting for him at every turn. The ragged mountains in the clear sunlight were a sight of breathtaking beauty but in the darkness of a snow-storm these same mountains could become a death trap.

Jan struggled cautiously on. Where his skis had been an advantage in the past, they were now a liability. He moved faster on them but now, almost blinded by the snow, he had no way of telling when he might dash clear over a cliff edge or into a gully, unable to stop quickly enough in his tracks. It was not long before the visibility became so poor that he was totally disorientated, unable to tell if he was travelling upwards or downwards or close to a precipitous cliff. By then he was like a snowman feeling his way through the storm and he was lost, hopelessly lost in a white hell. He considered taking shelter in the hope that the storm would soon abate but his mind was troubled by the thought that if he stopped he would die where he lay so he fought on, edging his way in which direction he did not know.

Baalsrud pressed on blindly through the storm, inching his way across the snow but the white surface beneath his feet was beginning to slide down the mountainside threatening to avalanche. His body ached from the strain and at last he came to a great rock. He knew then he could go no farther in the storm so he nestled beside it and lapsed into sleep, hoping that when he awoke he would find the storm had passed. But when he wakened he found the storm had grown in intensity. He had lost all sense of time and was overcome by a sense of futility.

It was not long after as he tried to make his way farther along the mountainside that near disaster struck. The snow beneath his feet began to move, slowly at first then with greater speed carrying him with it. The dull rumble of an avalanche reached his ears then mighty chunks of snow bounded down the mountainside, bowling him over. The whole mountain seemed to be on the move as the thundering roar of the avalanche grew, casting him downwards. His body was hammered by the falling snow as it was carried down the mountainside. The skis attached to his feet were shattered into fragments. In a second he would be enveloped in snow, smothered under its weight then as quickly he would be tossed out of it.

Finally, after what seemed like an eternity, he came to a halt in a valley with the life almost pounded out of him. He had fallen three hundred feet and he lay there in the snow, for how long no one knows. Most of his body was buried but mercifully his head was clear of the snow and he could at least breathe. This undoubtedly saved his life.

When he finally came to, he struggled from the snow, frozen to the marrow and took stock of his situation. It was decidedly grim. The storm was still raging violently and he hadn't the remotest idea of where he was. His senses were numbed by the merciless pounding his body had taken and now he had reached a point where it was only the subconscious will to survive which made him fight on. Instinct told him that he dared not rest for that would mean being frozen to death.

He had to keep moving and for the next *three days* he stumbled through the storm with his body becoming almost completely encased in ice. Even his veins began to freeze arresting the circulation in his body but Jan could feel nothing—nor could he see anything for by then he was totally blind. He was even completely unaware that the storm had ended when it eventually blew itself out on the third day and the sky cleared bringing with it the sun. For he could see nothing. He had reached such a state of unawareness that he might well have been dead for he knew nothing of what he was doing. He wandered aimlessly through the snow until at last he bumped into a huge, solid mass. By some miracle he had reached a house. He felt his way around it and fell in the open doorway.

Inside the house, the occupants, Hanna Pedersen and her two children, gazed in horror at the apparition which appeared before them. It resembled something from a vintage horror film with an almost zombie-like appearance, its head matted with blood and clothes frozen solid. Fru Pedersen ran from the house and found her brother Marius, who lived in the house next door. What Marius saw lying there was a man on the point of death. Who he was or where he had come from, he had no idea. The man talked in an incoherent garble none of which Marius could understand and it was pointless trying. The most important thing to do was to get some life back into the frozen body.

Marius Grönvold set about the task of getting the frozen clothes off Jan's body while his sister built up a roaring fire. Jan's clothes had to be cut off him and they revealed that his feet were frozen into solid blocks of ice and were black with frostbite. Jan was completely unaware of what was happening and could feel nothing even when Marius used the old Norwegian remedy for frostbite, rubbing the frozen limbs with snow.

Slowly the warmth of the fire and Marius' ministering of first aid began to restore life to Jan's body and he was able to answer Marius' questions. Even in his terrible state, Jan remembered to keep his true identity a secret. It had become second nature to him. He had been living a lie since he set foot in Norway. Marius realised that what the man was telling him was not the truth and to him that in itself confirmed he was no Nazi. He realised that a German sympathiser would not have to bluff his way out of the situation. With that Marius wrapped him in blankets, laid him on a bed and let him fall into a deep, warm sleep.

Marius had told Jan that he had reached Furuflaten, a small village on the edge of the mighty fifty-mile-long Lyngenfjord. What's more, he had not only reached it but passed through the town which was garrisoned by German troops. It was nothing short of miraculous that Jan had not been seen and that he had stumbled upon the house of a man whose loyalty to Norway was unquestionable. There was, however, a problem. Jan could not be kept in the house. In small outposts like Furuflaten, news travelled fast and the fewer people who knew of Jan's existence there, the safer he would be. Marius decided that he must be moved and he puzzled over where he could hide him. He knew that whatever the answer was, he could never hope to move him on his own so he recruited the help of two other villagers whom he knew to be absolutely trustworthy.

On the far side of the fjord was a small, deserted hut which nobody ever visited and Marius chose that as the hiding place. It was to take a long time before Jan would be in any fit state to make the journey over the plateau to the frontier. He had to get fit again before such a venture could be considered.

Thanks to the care given him by Marius and his sister life gradually began to return to Jan's body and with it came unbearable pain. But with hope of survival growing he was able to withstand the pain. One night, Marius and his two friends gently laid Jan on to an improvised stretcher and with Fru Pedersen acting as lookout, carried him from the house to a boat under the very noses of the Germans, then rowed him across the fjord to the hut.

In the hut they made him as comfortable as possible and gave him what food they could spare. Having done what they could, they left Jan alone with his thoughts and returned to the village trying to act as normally as possible. But beneath that apparent façade of normality, Marius and his helpers were at work, planning and scheming what was to be done with Jan. None of them, although they would not admit it at the time, held out much hope of his survival. It would take weeks for him to regain sufficient strength to even think about the journey over the plateau and then there was the question of who would take him. None of the people of the village knew the plateau sufficiently well to guide him across it to the frontier, even if it were only twenty-five miles away. Somehow they would have to enlist the aid of other patriots who knew the region and could undertake the journey.

While Marius and his friends puzzled over what was to be done with Jan, the sick man lay in darkness in the hut with his sight gradually returning to him. The hours passed slowly for him and he was in continuous pain from his feet. It was two nights later that Marius returned to visit Jan and bring him some more food. The sight of Marius was heartening for Jan who had begun to despair that he would ever see him again and when Marius left, Jan felt even more lonely than before.

Marius promised to return again as soon as he could but a violent storm broke out and it was five days before he came back to the hut. The sight that confronted him was one of horror. Jan was on the point of death. He was lying in his bunk having suffered unbelievable pain from his feet. Gangrene had set in and his toes had turned black. He was in a stupor from the pain. In a bid to relieve himself of the intense agony he had slashed his toes with a knife in the hope that letting out the blood would take with it the infection. It had not worked and had in fact drawn every ounce of strength from his body. He had lain there for days, unable to move and losing hope that anyone would come for him. He had resigned himself to death.

Such was Jan's perilous state that the situation had become even more desperate than before. There was no hope of finding a doctor to come to him or take him to hospital. Only in Sweden could he hope to get hospital treatment without the threat of discovery by the Germans but in his pitiful condition it seemed unlikely that he would survive the journey. Marius and his friends were, however, determined to try. It was his only hope.

Jan's spirits were at their lowest ebb and Marius saw that he had to revive them otherwise he might give way to death. He told Jan that already contact had been made with men in the village of Mandal who were willing to help in getting him across the plateau. He would be taken by sledge over the mountains to the village then taken on from there by the men from Mandal. This news had the desired effect and Jan's spirits rose.

It was three days before he saw Marius again and this time he brought with him three men, Amandus Lillevoll, Alvin Larsen and Olaf Lanes, all three of whom had volunteered to help get Jan across the mountain to Mandal. They brought with them a hastily built sledge, some blankets, food and a bottle of brandy.

The courage shown by these men in helping Jan was enormous. They would inevitably be away from the village for some time and they would be missed by the Germans who kept a close watch on their comings and goings. When they returned they would have to explain their absence and failure to come up with a convincing story might lead to the discovery of their connection with the fugitive, the penalty for which was death, not only for them but possibly for their families as well. When one considers that none of them really thought Jan would last the journey and the whole undertaking might all be in vain, their courage is all the greater.

Such then was the prospect facing the four men when they laid Jan on the sledge, strapped him on to it and began their journey over the mountain. They started off pulling and pushing the weighty sledge up the steep incline. The going was difficult and slow. With each step they took, they seemed to slide back on the slippery surface and they were strained to the limits of endurance but they battled on while Jan lay unconscious on the sledge for most of the time. At one point disaster almost struck when one of them stumbled and the sledge began to slide down the slope. As it careered down, however, it hit one of the men and stopped but not without half crushing the man's chest in the process. In spite of the near catastrophe, they struggled on and after an epic battle against the elements, they reached the top.

Marius had arranged that the men from Mandal would meet them at the foot of a bluff and they made for this, expecting to find the others waiting for them but when they arrived at the appointed meeting place there was no one there. The whole area was deserted. (It was later discovered that the men from Mandal dared not leave their homes because the Germans had carried out a lightning house-to-house search and the village was being closely watched.)

Marius and the others were now faced with a problem. What were they to do? They couldn't take Jan over the plateau and they could not go to Mandal. Perhaps, they thought, the others had been mistaken about the meeting place. Three of them went off in search of the men who should have been waiting for them but there was no sign of them. They were at a loss as to what they should do.

There was, of course, only one thing they could do and that was leave Jan and return to their homes. Jan knew this and so did the others. He insisted that they leave him in the hope that the Mandal men might find him. They had risked enough taking him as far as they had done and it was asking too much of a man to risk any more. The men hated the decision but it was the inevitable one and the right one to take, so with a few parting words of encouragement to Jan, they left with the promise that somehow or other a message would be got through to Mandal telling the men where he was and to pick him up the following night.

Now Jan was alone with only the snow and the stars for company. He was well wrapped up in the blankets but soon the cold began to creep into him. His body ached but he tried as best he could between bouts of unconsciousness to do exercises in his confined space to keep his circulation going. The following night came and with it a storm which brought heavy downfalls of snow. Throughout that night he lay there hoping against hope that his rescuers would come but they didn't and soon the blizzard enveloped Jan completely. He was entombed in a grave of snow ... and there he was to lie for *seven days*!

During that time the men from Mandal searched for him at night in the hope of finding him but they could not and it was not until Marius returned on the seventh night that Jan was dug out from his pit of snow. It was unbelievable but he was still alive. He had kept himself from death by sipping at the brandy and nibbling at the remains of the food Marius had left him. There he was nearer death than he had ever been but a sparkle came to his dark eyes when he saw Marius' face. He had brought with him more brandy and some food and this helped revive Jan.

The men from Mandal had assumed that by then Jan would be dead and now Marius had to get in touch with them and tell them he was still alive and the planned escape must go ahead with all speed. To do this, Marius had to leave but he stuck a marker in the snow to direct the searching men.

It was two nights later that Jan heard the calls of the men who had struggled through the snow for him. At last they found him and dragged him from the pit in which he lay. Jan could not believe his eyes. He had given up all hope of rescue but now they had come and they told him they were to attempt a crossing of the flat, windswept plateau that very day.

The group of men set off pulling Jan's sledge but the weather deteriorated to such an extent that they had to turn back and they headed for the mountain on the other side of Mandal. There they built a snow house for Jan and left him with food, promising to return as soon as the storm abated. The excitement felt by Jan, even in his frail condition, was great. At last he was on the last lap of his journey and escape was within sight—but the last lap was to prove as agonising as the others.

Jan lay in the snow house for two nights before the men returned with food and medicine. They told him they had arranged that a Lapp, one of the wandering tribes of herdsmen who roam the arctic wilds, was to come for him and take him across the frontier. This was, they said, by far the safest way to cross the frontier for the Lapp knew the country and furthermore would not arouse suspicion by his presence there. Jan waited patiently for the Lapp but he did not come—in fact he never came but the men of Mandal returned night after night to feed and tend to Jan.

Time dragged on until one night the men arrived to tell him that the Germans had returned to their village and were searching it. He had to be moved and he was taken to a cave which was warm and dry. He lay in that cave for no less than twenty-three days while the gangrene ate away at his toes until they eventually all rotted away. Only the nightly visits of his friends reassured him and gave him the determination to fight on.

Finally a plan was evolved with the help of men from a nearby valley who agreed to arrange a crossing for Jan. He was taken from his hide-out by eight men from Mandal and carried for thirteen hours over the mountain until they were met by two men. Jan was left with them, then the wait began for another Lapp who had promised to take him across the frontier. But again he was let down when they heard that the Lapp was ill and could not come. It seemed that Jan was destined never to cross the frontier but as luck would have it another Lapp passed their way en route to his herd of reindeer which was near the frontier. He agreed to take care of Jan. He was transferred to the Lapp's reindeer sledge and they set off.

For two days the Lapp drove the sledge on across the plateau but trouble was waiting for them. Within sight of the frontier, they saw a German ski patrol. There was no hope of calling their bluff. The Germans knew who they were and fired at the Lapp and his sledge but they were well out of range, then with one last frantic dash, they swept over the frontier into Finland. However, Jan was not yet out of danger. Finland was fighting on the side of the Germans. They still had to reach sanctuary in Sweden. Luckily in that desolate land they encountered no opposition and at last they came to a frozen lake which they crossed into Sweden. Jan Baalsrud had made good his escape from the Germans. With his courage and that of the many people who had risked their lives to help him, he had foxed the Germans. He had crossed the frontier on 1 June. The manhunt had lasted for almost two and a half months.

Jan Baalsrud recovered from his terrible wounds and condition in hospital and eventually found his way back to England. Throughout the remaining war years the story of Jan's epic escape spread throughout Norway and his courage became an inspiration to those who lived under the Nazi terror.

*BIBLIOGRAPHY*

During the course of his research into the subject of wartime escape, the author referred to many books for background information and technical detail. Some of those books listed below were the main sources and are recommended to the reader who wishes to delve deeper into the subject.

Brickhill, Paul. *Escape or Die.* New York: W. W. Norton; London: Evans Brothers, 1952.

——, and Norton, Conrad. *Escape to Danger.* London: Faber and Faber.

Burt, Kendal, and Leasor, James. *The One That Got Away.* London: Wm. Collins, 1956.

Crawley, Aidan. *Escape from Germany.* London: Wm. Collins.

Eggers, Reinhold. *Colditz.* London: Robert Hale, 1961.

Evans, A. J. *The Escaping Club.* London: Jonathan Cape, 1921.

Howarth, David. *We Die Alone.* New York: Macmillan; London: Wm. Collins, 1955.

Williams, Eric. *The Wooden Horse.* New York: Dell, 1968; London: Wm. Collins, 1949.